A Simple Gl

The Catholic Church ı
which have a clear meanıng to Cauiones, or to mes
but can be puzzling to others. This word-list is intended to
explain some of these words and usages. It is not meant as a
substitute for the *Catholic Encyclopaedia*, or for theological and
Scriptural dictionaries, although inevitably some terms used in
theology are included; but it might help clear up confusion.
Words relating to the Church of the past have also been
included, because even if the things they describe (like *Prime* or
maniples) are at present not in use, readers will benefit from a
degree of completeness especially if reading older books or
accounts of older events. Obviously, no booklet this size can
pretend to be comprehensive; but we have tried to include all
the obvious words, and also some others of particular interest. It
is meant to be not primarily a glossary of "hard words" but of
commonly used terms. There are some words (*apocrypha*,
attrition, *chapter*, *fraction*) which have a meaning in general
usage that differs from the special sense they bear for Catholics.
These too have been covered. Some Catholic expressions
(*devil's advocate*, *moveable feast*) have passed, modified, into
general usage; their original meaning is given below.

Headwords are given in **bold**; where this might be helpful, or
interesting, etymologies are then given in brackets, with
cognates in *ITALIC CAPITALS*; words within definitions that
occur elsewhere in this glossary are given in *italics*.

A

Abba (Aramaic, "father") Familiar name used by Jesus for God, his Father; later the affectionate title given to senior *monks* in Egypt; from this derives **Abbot**, the superior of a *monastery* of men, and **Abbess**, the equivalent for women. In either case the monastery can be called an **Abbey**.

Absolution (Latin *ABSOLUTIO*, from *ABSOLVO*, "set free") The solemn pronouncement by a *priest* in the *Sacrament* of Penance (*Confession*) that someone's sins are forgiven.

Abstinence (Latin *ABSTINENTIA*, from *ABSTINEO*, "hold back, refrain") Not eating meat; a form of *penance* now obligatory in England and Wales only on *Ash Wednesday* and *Good Friday*, and binding only on those between the ages of 14 and 65. In the past, Catholics were bound to abstain from meat on every Friday throughout the year. In some countries this is still the custom. Eating fish instead of meat on days of abstinence is a traditional, not obligatory, practice, one which finds Scriptural support in John 21:9-14.

Acolyte (Greek *AKOLUTES*, "follower") Originally, the fourth grade of *Holy Orders*, now suspended in the Latin Church. Now used for a lay ministry, assistant to the *priest*, hardly ever conferred except for those on the way to *ordination* as *deacon* or priest. Also used more loosely to refer to those who serve at *Mass*.

Act A movement of the will and heart towards God, hence an impulse in *prayer*. Specifically acts can mean short prayers designed to express the will to some virtue, most commonly an *Act of Contrition*; Acts of Faith, Hope and Charity are also found in prayer-books.

Ad limina (Latin, "to the threshold [of the Apostles]") Technical term for the regular visits (usually every five years) made by diocesan *bishops* to the *Holy See.*

Adoration Worship directed to God; often especially used in the phrase *Eucharistic Adoration.*

Advent (Latin *ADVENTUS*, "arrival") The season before *Christmas*, celebrating the coming of Christ to earth at Bethlehem, and in the *Church*, and looking forward to the *Parousia*; traditionally a time of *penance.*

Agape (Greek, "brotherly love, charity") A technical term for the unselfish love the Christian is enabled to have towards God and neighbour, modelled on the complete self-giving of the *Holy Trinity*; also, in the *New Testament* and *Church Fathers*, a "love feast" (shared meal) that accompanied or followed the *Eucharist.*

Agnus Dei (Latin, "lamb of God") A text (referring to Jesus as the true *Passover* sacrifice) used just before *Communion* at *Mass*, to coincide with the *fraction*, often set to music.

Alb (Latin *[TUNICA* or *VESTIS] ALBA* "white garment") The second of the *vestments* for *Mass*, a full-length sleeved white gown. Sometimes also worn by those serving Mass.

Alleluia (Hebrew, "praise God!") An interjection found frequently in *Scripture* and the *liturgy*; hence, **Alleluia verse**, a joyous chant sung just before the *Gospel* at *Mass*, except during *Lent*. The spelling Hallelujah attempts to be closer to the Hebrew pronunciation of the word, and is characteristic of Protestant usage.

All Saints A *Solemnity* on 1st November each year to commemorate the countless saints, known and unknown, who have no particular *feast-day*. Formerly called All Hallows (Old English *HĀLGA* "saint"). The vigil of the feast, October 31st, was known as Halloween (All Hallows' Eve). Once a pre-Christian pagan festival, it has since become a secular event of no religious significance.

All Souls A commemoration on 2nd November of all those who have died, when the Christian has a particular duty to pray for their souls.

Almsgiving Practical charitable donations to those in need, of either money or goods.

Almuce (Medieval Latin *ALMUCIA*) A *mozzetta*; sometimes explained as a Middle English variant of the word *amice*, although this is unclear.

Altar (Latin *ALTARE*, *ALTARIUM*, sg of *ALTARIA* "burnt offerings", prob from *ADOLERE* "burn in sacrifice". The frequently supposed connexion with *ALTUS* "high" is factitious) A strong oblong flat raised surface, ideally of stone on a stone base, used for the Sacrifice of the *Mass*. It is "dressed" with three white **altar-cloths**, running its full length and hanging down at the ends, and an **altar-frontal**, covering the side facing the people, properly of the colour of the *liturgical season*.

Altar-bread Unleavened bread, often in the form of wafers, used for the *Eucharist*.

Altar Missal, see *Missal*, *Sacramentary*.

Altar-rails Low railings of metal, stone or wood, found in some churches, serving to demarcate the *sanctuary*, and to provide support for those kneeling to receive *Communion*.

Altar of Repose A *side altar*, or a specially constructed occasional altar, decorated to serve as a place of reservation of the *Blessed Sacrament* for the evening of *Maundy Thursday*.

Ambo (Greek *AMBON*, "pulpit", perhaps from *ANABAINO*, "go up steps") A raised platform in the *sanctuary* where the *Gospel* is proclaimed; also sometimes used for preaching from. Originally a term from the Greek-speaking Church of the East. See also *Lectern*.

Amice (Latin *AMICTUS* "cloak", or medieval Latin *AMICIA*) The first of the *vestments* for *Mass*, a neck-cloth to keep the *alb* clean and cover the priest's collar. See *almuce*.

Anamnesis (Greek, "calling to mind, remembrance") New Testament term describing the narrative parts of the *Eucharistic Prayer*, which make present the Last Supper and the sacrifice of Jesus on Calvary.

Anastasis (Greek, "raising up, resurrection) The Resurrection; also, the name of the original Church of the Holy Sepulchre.

Anaphora (Greek, "offering, lifting up") Another name for the *Eucharistic Prayer*.

Anathema (Greek, "an accursed thing") Historically, a term used by *ecumenical councils* to describe *heresies* formally condemned.

Anchorites (Medieval Latin *ANCHORITA*, Greek *ANAKHŌRETES* from *ANAKHOREIN* "to retire, withdraw") Those who live lives of complete solitude devoted to prayer, remaining in a single place for life. (Now rare.)

Angel (Greek, *ANGELOS*, "messenger") A pure spirit, created by God to praise and worship Him; some have the particular mission of being intermediary between God and man. Traditionally divided into nine orders or hierarchies (*angels*, *archangels*, virtues, dominations, principalities, powers, thrones, *cherubim*, *seraphim*) although these categories are not a *dogma*. See *Archangel*, *Guardian Angel*, *cherub*, *seraph*.

Angelus (Latin "angel") A prayer commemorating the *annunciation* by the *angel* Gabriel to Mary, traditionally said at six in the morning, midday and six in the evening; hence the **Angelus Bell** which is rung at those times.

Anima Christi (Latin, "soul of Christ") A traditional prayer, of medieval date, famously used by St Ignatius in his *Spiritual Exercises*.

Annulment A declaration by the *Church* that a particular marriage never in fact took place, owing to a previously undeclared defect of form or intention.

Annunciation (Latin *ANNUNTIATIO* from *ANNUNTIO*, "announce") A *Solemnity* on 25th March to commemorate the announcement of the Angel to Mary that she would give birth to Jesus (*Lk* 1:26-38); during Christian times was kept as the first day of the year; known in England as *Lady Day*.

Anointing Smearing blessed oil on the skin, usually on the forehead, as a sign of healing and strengthening. Used in *Baptism* and *Confirmation*, in the *Ordination* of priests and bishops, and *Anointing of the Sick*, all of which are *Sacraments*.

Anointing of the Sick A *sacrament* for healing, which should be given at the onset of any serious illness, and may be repeated.

Antiphon (Greek *ANTI* "opposite", *PHONÉ* "sound, voice") A verse usually derived from *Scripture*, sung or said before and after every *psalm* and *canticle* in the *Divine Office*, varying according to the day and season. Hence **Antiphonale**, a book containing the chants for the antiphons and the rest of the Office.

Apocalypse (Greek, *APOKALUPSIS*, "revelation") A text recording a vision or figurative prophecy, often of the End Times; without further qualification, it generally refers to the Scriptural Book of Revelation of St John.

Apocrypha (Greek *APOKRUPHA*, "things hidden or concealed" from *APOKRUPTO* "to hide from view, conceal") Jewish and early Christian books omitted from the *Canon of Scripture*. (i) In Catholic usage, the apocrypha (or **apocryphal books**) means various texts (Enoch, Jubilees, the Shepherd of Hermas amongst many others) of varied provenance which are not accepted in any version of the Bible; (ii) in Protestant usage, the apocrypha (sometimes called the Deuterocanonical books) refers to a number of books and parts of books (Maccabees, Wisdom, Judith, parts of Daniel and others) found in the Catholic and Orthodox Bibles but omitted for various reasons by Protestant Bibles from the sixteenth century onwards, or included only as an appendix.

Apologetics Reasoned defence of the truths of the Faith, especially against the arguments of objectors. Cf 1 *P* 3:15.

Apostasy (Greek, *APOSTASIS*, "defection"; *APOSTATES*, "deserter") Deliberate formal rejection of the Catholic faith; one who so rejects the faith is an **apostate**.

Apostle (Greek, *APOSTOLOS*, "messenger, envoy" from *APOSTELLO*, "I send") One of the twelve men chosen from amongst Jesus's *disciples* to be his particular representatives, especially after the *Ascension*. Whilst all Apostles are disciples, not all disciples are Apostles. See *Disciple*.

Apostolic Delegate The diplomatic representative of the *Holy See* to a particular sovereign state. See *Nuncio*.

Apostolic Succession The *doctrine* that the line of *bishops* (and thus of *priests*) descends in an unbroken chain from the *Apostles*.

Apostolic Tradition The *Church's* belief that the faith she passes on comes down from the *Apostles* in an unbroken succession guaranteed by the *Holy Spirit*; and that the *Scriptures* can only properly be proclaimed and interpreted within the Church. Although the words and formulae used to express the Church's faith have often been refined and developed over time, Apostolic Tradition means that this fullness of belief is already latent from the very earliest Christian times, being entrusted to the Apostles and their successors by Jesus Christ himself.

Archangel A chief or ruling angel. Three archangels are named in Scripture: Michael, Raphael, Gabriel. Other supposed archangels are named in *apocryphal* writings, but these form no part of the Christian faith.

Archbishop The *bishop* of an important *diocese* who acts as leader of a group of dioceses or Province; Also known as a *metropolitan*.

Archdeacon Originally, the senior *deacon* of a *diocese* often delegated by the *bishop* to represent him; these functions are now exercised by the *vicar general*. Retained as an honorific title for some European cathedral *clergy*, and amongst Anglicans.

Archdiocese A *diocese* governed by an *Archbishop*.

Archpriest A title sometimes given to a senior *priest* (*dean*) at a *cathedral*; historically, a priest with authority over other priests in the absence of a *bishop*.

Ascension The event when Jesus "withdrew from them [his apostles] and was carried up to heaven" some time after his resurrection (*Ac* 1:6-11). **Ascension Thursday**, forty days after *Easter*, is the *Solemnity* commemorating this.

Ashes The dust of burnt palms often mixed with water and smeared on the foreheads of the faithful as a sign of accepting *penance* at the beginning of *Lent*. Hence **Ash Wednesday**, the first day of Lent, six and a half weeks before *Easter*.

Asperges (Latin, "You will sprinkle") A chant accompanying the sprinkling of the *congregation* with *holy water* at the start of a traditional *High Mass*; often used as a shorthand term for this ceremony at Mass on Sundays or *feast-days*.

Aspergillum (Latin, "holy water sprinkler") Something used to sprinkle *holy water*: a sprig of greenery, a brush, or a metal dispenser.

Assumption The *dogma* that the *Virgin Mary* was assumed bodily into heaven at the end of her earthly life, traditionally at Ephesus in Asia Minor: a sign and promise that our own redemption will also be bodily; commemorated by a *Solemnity* on 15th August.

Attrition (Latin *ATTRITIO*, from *ATTERO* "wear away") Sorrow for sins arising from fear of punishment. See *Contrition*.

Augustinians Members of a family of *friars* and *nuns* inspired by the example of St Augustine; also most communities of *Canons Regular* following a Rule based on St Augustine's writings.

Auxiliary Bishop A *bishop* appointed to assist the principal bishop of an especially large *diocese*. See *Co-Adjutor*.

Ave Maria (Latin, "Hail, Mary") See *Hail Mary*.

B

Baldacchino (Italian, "from Baghdad", traditionally the source of richly embroidered fabrics: hence "canopy", originally made of such fabric) Architectural term for a stone-built canopy over an *altar*, often curtained around. Also called a *Ciborium*.

Baptism (Greek *BAPTISMOS*, from *BAPTIZO*, "dip, immerse") Dipping water and pouring it over the head, or immersing the person in water: the *sacrament* by which *catechumens* are incorporated into the life of the *Church*, die to their old nature, and are reborn in Christ. The Church baptizes babies on the understanding that their parents and *godparents* undertake the duty of handing on faith to them.

Baptism of the Lord A *Solemnity* kept on the Sunday after *Epiphany* to commemorate the *baptism* of Jesus in the Jordan.

Baptistery The area of a *church* used for *baptism*, containing the *font*; often a demarcated space near the main door.

Basil, Liturgy of Saint One of the three Eucharistic liturgies commonly used by the *Orthodox Church*.

Basilica (Late Latin, from Greek *BASILIKE* "a royal building, palace" from *BASILEUS* "king") Originally, a large public hall like the audience chamber of a royal palace. Many such were used as *churches* from the fourth century onwards. Some older or especially notable newer churches retain, or have been granted, the honorific title of basilica.

Beatification An official declaration by the *Church* that a particular man or woman, who has lived a life of heroic Christian virtue and to whose intercession a posthumous miracle has been attributed, may be publicly venerated (at *Mass*, with readings for the *Divine Office* &c) in a particular country or region, and should now be titled "*Blessed*". See *Canonization*.

Beatitudes (Latin, *BEATITUDO* "happiness" from *BEATUS* "happy, blessed") (i) The eight sayings of Jesus explaining the nature of true happiness (see *Mt* 5:3-10); (ii) in the singular, the happiness of the *saints* in heaven.

Benedicite (Latin, "bless ye") See *Canticle of Daniel*.

Benedictines *Monks* and *nuns* following the Rule of St Benedict, usually wearing black.

Benediction (Latin *BENEDICTIO* "blessing") A service of worship centred around the *Blessed Sacrament*, exposed on the *altar* in a *monstrance*; may be accompanied by hymns, silent prayer, *Scripture* reading or the *Divine Office*.

Benedictus (Latin "blessed") (i) The Canticle of Zechariah (*Lk* 1:68-79), used at *Lauds*; (ii) the second half of the *Sanctus*, sometimes detached and set to music separately.

Bidding Prayers (Old English *BIDDAN*, "to ask, entreat") Term used in England for the *Prayer of the Faithful*, intercessions made after the *sermon* at *Mass*.

Biretta (Italian *BERETTA*, Spanish *BIRETTA*, from medieval Latin *BIRETTUM* "cap", diminutive of late Latin *BIRRUS*, "hooded cape") A square stiff cap with three wings on top, formerly worn by *clergy* in the *sanctuary* (it is not street dress); red for *cardinals*, purple for *prelates*, black for others; now rare. *Secular* clergy have a pom-pom on top of it. To be distinguished from **Beretta**, a make of Italian handgun.

Bishop (Old English *BISCOP*, from vulgar Latin **(E)BISCOBUS*, aphetic form of *EPISCOPUS*, Greek *EPISKOPOS*, "overseer") A *priest* chosen and consecrated or ordained to administer a *diocese*, and to confer *confirmation* and *ordination*.

Bishops' Conference Originally a meeting of all the *bishops* of a particular nation or region; now generally refers to the bureaucratic structures originally established to support these meetings and subsequent co-ordinated action by bishops but which now operate with some degree of autonomy.

Blackfriars Traditional English name for *Dominican friars*.

Blessed See *beatification*.

Blessed Sacrament Generally, the *Eucharist*; particularly used to refer to the consecrated *Host* reserved as a focus for devotion - such as *contemplative prayer* before the *Tabernacle*, in processions, at *Benediction* and so on.

Blessed Virgin Mary See *Our Lady*.

Breviary (Latin *BREVIARIUM* "summary, abridgement") A book containing all the texts for the *Divine Office*.

Bull (Latin *BULLA*, "seal") A formal document from the *Pope* making a declaration of some importance, sealed with a lead seal.

Burse (French *BOURSE*, Latin *BURSA* "purse") A square fabric-covered container for the *corporal*, not now always used, but if it is, it should match the *chalice-veil* and *chasuble*.

C

Camaldolese (from Camaldoli in Italy, its place of foundation) An order of *monks* living strictly as *hermits* within a community, founded by St Romuald.

Candlemas Traditional English name for the feast of the *Purification* of Mary, or the *Presentation of the Lord*, on 2nd February. Patronal feast of Oriel College, Oxford.

Canon (Greek *KANON*, "rule") (i) A decree on some matter of *Church* order or discipline passed by the *Pope* or a *General Council* which is binding on the Church unless revoked by the same authority, collected into the **Code of Canon Law**, and interpreted by **Canon Lawyers**; (ii) derived from the above, originally a man whose way of life is regulated by the canons, hence one of a community of *priests*; later divided into **Canons Regular** who take vows and live almost like *monks*, and **Canons Secular** who can own their own property. These formed communities at *cathedrals*, so that the title Canon came to mean one of the senior cathedral *clergy*, now often given as an honorary title; (iii) the central prayer of the *Mass*, or *Eucharistic Prayer*; (iv) **Canon of Scripture**, the complete list of 72 (or 73 if Jeremiah and Lamentations are counted as two) books included in sacred *Scripture* by the *Apostolic Tradition*.

Canonization An *infallible* declaration by the *Pope* that a particular Christian who has previously been *beatified* is worthy of universal veneration as a *saint*; for this, evidence of a second posthumous miracle is required. See *beatification*.

Canopy (Latin *CANOPEUM*, *CONOPEUM* "mosquito net" from Greek *KONOPEION*, "bed fitted with mosquito nets") A fabric shade carried on four poles over the *Blessed Sacrament* during outdoor *processions*, e.g. on *Corpus Christi*.

Canticle (Latin *CANTICULUM*, diminutive of *CANTICUM*, "chant") Short verse-like passages from *Scripture* found together with *psalms* in the *Divine Office*.

Canticle of Daniel In full, the Song of the Three Young Men from the Book of Daniel (*Dn* 3:52-90); in common usage, either of two extracts from it used at Sunday *Lauds*: the longer (*Dn* 3:57-88, 56 also called the *Benedicite*) and the shorter (*Dn* 3:52-57) are found on alternate Sundays.

Cantor (Latin, "singer") Originally one of the minor *Holy Orders* conferring a particular responsibility for singing during the *liturgy*; now typically used to refer to *laypeople* with this responsibility.

Cardinal (Latin *CARDINALIS* (from *CARDO*, "hinge"), "attached [to a particular church] like a hinge to a door") A senior dignitary of the *Church*, one of the College who elect a new *Pope* after the death of his predecessor. Technically they do this as senior *clergy* of the Diocese of Rome electing their *bishop*; for this reason each Cardinal is assigned a titular church within the Diocese of Rome. Cardinals are now usually *Archbishops*, either resident in Rome and working within the *Curia*, or governing their *dioceses* throughout the world.

Cardinal Virtues Prudence, justice, fortitude and temperance.

Carmelites Members of a large family of *friars* and *nuns* inspired by the example of the early hermits on Mount Carmel in Palestine, and the Prophet Elijah, with a strong tradition of *prayer*. The friars were known in England as *Whitefriars* because of the white outer cloaks they wear in public.

Carthusians (Latin *CARTHUSIANUS* "a man of Chartreuse") An order of *monks* and *nuns* founded by St Bruno, living strictly as *hermits* but within a community. See *Charterhouse*.

Cassock (French *CASAQUE*, Italian *CASSACA* "type of long coat" from Turkish *QUZZAK*, *KAZAK* Russian *KOZAK*, *KAZAK* "nomad, vagabond, cossack" thence transf. to the type of riding-coat worn by them) A full-length sleeved garment, buttoned down the front, worn as the foundation garment for *vestments*, and in many religious communities as the ordinary house dress.

May be girded with a *fascia*. Colours of fabric, buttons and fascia vary according to rank; white for the *Pope*, red for *Cardinals*, purple for *bishops* and *monsignors*; otherwise black. Also called a *soutane*.

Catechesis Oral teaching of the Christian faith, given by a *catechist*.

Catechism A systematic body of instruction in the Christian faith, often in a question-and-answer form.

Catechist One who gives oral instruction in the Christian faith ("catechizes", from Greek *KATAKHIZEIN*, *KATAKHEIN* "to instruct orally") or *catechesis*.

Catechumen Generally, anyone receiving *catechesis* or under instruction from *catechists*; specifically, a new convert to Christianity who is under instruction but has not yet been *baptized*. Hence **Catechumenate**, the period of instruction for new Christians, in the early *Church* often extended over months or years but now typically much briefer (see *RCIA*).

Catenians (Latin *CATENA*, "chain") An association of Catholic men (often working in the professions or in business) and their wives, who meet for mutual support, *prayer*, and charitable purposes. It was founded in Manchester in 1908, and counts 11,000 members worldwide.

Cathedral (Latin *CATHEDRALIS* (adj) from Greek *KATHEDRA*, "seat") The mother *church* of a *diocese* where the *bishop* takes his seat; usually but not necessarily a large church. Originally an abbreviation for **Cathedral Church**.

Catholic Truth Society An independent Catholic charity and publisher founded in 1868 to promote the understanding and practice of the faith.

Catholic Womens' League (CWL) An association of women devoted to *evangelization* and practical works of charity.

Celibacy (Latin *CÆLIBATUS* from *CÆLEBS*, "bachelor") Strictly, the state of not (yet) being married, but by extension the condition of *priests*, *monks*, *friars* and *nuns*, and all who are committed to remaining unmarried.

Cenacle (Latin *CENACULUM*, "supper room") Name for the room in Jerusalem where, by tradition, Jesus and his *disciples* ate the Last Supper.

Censer (Anglo-Norman form of Old French *CENSIER*, aphetic form of *ENCENSIER* from *ENCENS* "incense") A metal container suspended from chains, used for burning *incense*. Also called a *thurible*.

Ceremonial of Bishops A book containing the various rites and ceremonies peculiar to *bishops*.

Chalice (Latin *CALIX*, "cup") A cup of gold or gilt silver, used for the wine which is to be *consecrated* at *Mass*.

Chant, Gregorian A type of slow solemn usually unaccompanied vocal music, traditionally used for texts from the *Mass* and *Divine Office*. Developed in western *monasteries* from the tenth century onwards on a basis of various earlier Christian and Jewish vocal traditions, it is called Gregorian after Pope Gregory the Great (ob.604), whose association with it is however unproven.

Chapel (late Latin *CAPELLA*, originally a diminutive of *CAPPA* (cf *cope*) meaning "little cloak", hence a name for the shrine at Aix where the cloak of St Martin of Tours was kept as a relic; hence any section of a large church with a particular function or dedication) Either a partially separated section of a *church* with an *altar* in it (*side altar* in *side chapel*), or a free-standing building which does not serve a *parish* but only a small community.

Chaplet (Old French *CHAPELET*, "wreath for the head") A loop of beads, on which various forms of prayer can be recited, the best-known being the *Rosary*.

Chapter Originally (i) the daily meeting of *monks* at which one chapter of the Rule was read before business; later (ii) similar meetings of *canons*; hence (iii) the business of the meeting itself, and (iv) the canons seen as a legislative body.

Charism (Greek *KHARISMA*, "grace, favour") A gift of the *Holy Spirit* given to a specific person for a specific purpose; hence the sense of purpose and spiritual identity of that person, or of a group of persons such as a *Religious Order*.

Charterhouse (Middle English version of French place name, Chartreuse, earlier Charteuse, near Grenoble) A monastery of *Carthusians*.

Chastity The virtue of sexual self-restraint. For the married this means fidelity to their spouse, with due respect for each other and the law of God. For the unmarried this means *continence*: abstaining from deliberate sexual activity.

Chasuble (late Latin *CASUBLA* "hooded cloak") The sixth of the *vestments* for Mass, an all-enveloping sleeveless garment which covers the others as a symbol of charity. It forms a set with the *stole* etc, and is of different colours for different *seasons*.

Cherub, pl **Cherubim** (Hebrew *KHERUB, KHERUBIM*) One of the orders of angels recognized by tradition. See *seraph, angel*.

Child of Prague See *Infant of Prague*.

Chrism (Greek *KHRISMA* from *KHRIEIN*, "to anoint") The mixture of oil and balsam (or similar aromatic) used for *anointing* in some ceremonies (*baptism, confirmation, ordination*, the dedication of a *church*). Blessed once a year by the *bishop* at a special **Chrism Mass** (usually during *Holy Week*).

Christ (Greek *CHRISTOS* "anointed one", translating Hebrew *MĀSIAH* "anointed one, Messiah") Common Catholic way of referring to Jesus, *Our Lord*.

Christ the King The last Sunday before *Advent*, a *Solemnity* to remind us that no earthly king or government can claim our loyalty, above Christ our true King.

Christening Traditional English term for *Baptism*, stressing that the person being baptized is now a Christian.

Christmas The *Solemnity* commemorating the birth of Jesus at Bethlehem, lasting throughout the *Octave* of Christmas, the eight days until 1st January; the **Christmas Season** continues until the Sunday after *Epiphany*, although it formerly extended for forty days until *Candlemas* (2 February).

Chrysostom, Liturgy of St John One of the three Eucharistic liturgies commonly used by the *Orthodox Church*.

Church (Old English *ÇIRIÇE* from Greek *KURIAKON*, "the Lord's place") (i) The entire community of all faithful Christians, united through space and time, with the *Pope* as the earthly focus of unity, and Christ alone as head. Formed by the *Eucharist*, and thus (like it) sometimes called the *Mystical Body of Christ*. There can only be one Church in this sense of the word; (ii) a "local" church as expression of the universal Church, with the *bishop* as focus of unity; effectively the same as a *diocese*; (iii) a building set aside and consecrated to be used for worship alone.

Church Fathers See *Fathers of the Church*.

Ciborium (Latin "drinking-cup" from Greek *KIBORION*, in medieval Latin wrongly supposed to be related to *CIBUM*, "food") (i) An airtight container, usually shaped like a covered cup, for the *Blessed Sacrament*; used to contain *hosts* during *Mass*, before and after their *consecration*, and reserved in the *Tabernacle*; (ii) architectural term for a stone-built canopy over an *altar*, often curtained around; also known as a *baldacchino*.

Cincture (Latin *CINCTURA*, "girding") The third of the *vestments* for *Mass*, a doubled cord to gird up the *alb* and hold the *stole* in place.

Circumcision The former name for the *Solemnity* on 1st January, reminding us that Jesus was a Jew in obedience to the Law. Also known as the *Octave* day of Christmas; now as the *Solemnity* of Mary, *Mother of God*.

Cistercians (Latin *CISTERCIENSIS* "from Cîteaux", a monastery near Dijon in France) *Monks* and *nuns* following the Rule of St Benedict in a strict manner, centrally organized; wearing white.

Clergy (Old French *CLERGÉ*, from Latin *CLERICATUS* "the body of clerks") Those men chosen by God to serve Him and His people, set aside by *ordination*, and with various duties and responsibilities.

Clergyman (i) a *cleric* or *clerk;* (ii) a term for the usual dress of secular priests (dark suit, shirt with clerical collar).

Cleric See *Clerk*.

Clerk (Old English from Latin *CLERICUS*, Greek *KLERIKOS* "clergyman", from *KLÉROS*, "lot") A *cleric*, man in *Holy Orders*; **Clerks Regular** are members of a religious order which has vows, but also a mission to the world, such as the *Jesuits*. In the middle ages anyone educated would likely be a cleric, hence clerk comes to mean also "scholar, educated man" and eventually "office worker".

Co-adjutor A *bishop* appointed to assist the bishop of a *diocese* in case of illness or incapacity; he has the right of succession to that *see* when it eventually falls vacant.

Collect A prayer led by the *priest* to collect or gather together the intentions of the people; in the *Mass* it comes after the *Kyrie* and *Gloria*.

Colours, Liturgical The *vestments* for *Mass* vary in colour according to the *liturgical season*. Particular seasons have their own colours; whilst particular classes of *feast-day* are so marked also. The main colours are: violet for *Advent* and *Lent*; white for *Christmas* and *Easter*; red for *Pentecost* and the feasts of *martyrs*. Rose-pink vestments may be worn on the *Gaudete Sunday* and *Laetare Sunday*; and black may be worn for funerals (*Requiem Masses*) and on *All Souls'* Day.

Commandments, Ten The foundation of the moral law of the *Old Testament* (see Exodus 20). Also called the *Decalogue*.

Commandments of the Church Six obligations binding on all Catholics: to keep Sundays and *Holy Days of Obligation* holy by hearing *Mass* and resting from work; observing the appointed days of *penance*; to go to *Confession*, and receive *Communion*, at least once a year (see *Easter Duties*); to contribute to the support of the *clergy*; and not to marry within certain degrees of kindred.

Communion, Holy The act of receiving and consuming the Body and Blood of Christ under the form of the consecrated *Host* and the consecrated wine, usually at *Mass*. See *Eucharist*.

Communion of Saints The unity and mutual solidarity of all Christians living and dead, forming the *Church*.

Communion verse A text sung while *Communion* is being distributed at *Mass*.

Compline or *Night Prayer*, the last hour of the *Divine Office* at the end of the day.

Concelebration The practice of two or more *priests* joining together to celebrate the *Eucharist* simultaneously.

Conclave (Latin *CONCLAVĒ* from *CUM CLAVE,* "with a key") The "locked-up" assembly of *Cardinals* charged with electing a new *Pope.*

Confession Admitting guilt and asking forgiveness for sins, the necessary precondition for receiving *absolution* in the *Sacrament of Penance.*

Confessor (i) A *priest* who hears *confession* in the *Sacrament* of *Penance*; (ii) a *saint* who is not a *martyr* but "confesses" his faith by the example of his life; e.g. St Edward, King and Confessor, so-called to distinguish him from his great uncle St Edward, King and Martyr.

Confirmation The *sacrament*, conferred by *anointing* on the forehead, that strengthens the Christian and brings to fulfilment the *gifts of the Holy Spirit* given in *baptism*; properly conferred by a *bishop.*

Congregation (Latin *CONGREGATIO*, "flocking together") (i) A gathering of people in a *church*, usually for worship; (ii) a community e.g. of *priests* living together; (iii) a major department or *dicastery* of the *Holy See*, usually based in the *Vatican City.*

Congregation for the Doctrine of the Faith (CDF) The *dicastery* of the Holy See responsible for accurate teaching of Catholic *doctrine*, and with investigating complaints against teachers or writers who distort the faith. Formerly called the Roman *Inquisition*, subsequently the *Holy Office*; since 1965 called the CDF.

Consecrate (Latin *CONSECRARE*, var. of *CON-SACRARE*, "make altogether holy") The act of handing over some person or thing over to God for His exclusive use. Hence **Consecration**, the central part of the *Mass*, when the bread and wine are consecrated to form the *Eucharist*.

Consistory (Latin *CONSISTORIUM* "council chamber" from *CONSISTO* "stand still, remain") A meeting of *Cardinals* with the *Pope*, particularly when new Cardinals are created.

Contemplation A form of mental *prayer* without words and without thought; being still in the presence of God. "He looks at me and I look at Him." Hence **Contemplative**, particularly applied to members of *religious orders* devoted to prayer.

Continence Refraining from deliberate sexual activity, as is expected of the unmarried.

Contrition (Latin *CONTRITIO* "sorrow") True sorrow for sin arising from the love of God.

Contrition, Act of A formal statement of sorrow for one's sins, and undertaking to avoid them in future, made during *confession* or on another occasion.

Convent (Latin *CONVENTUS*, "assembly, community") A religious community house; in England mainly used for houses of female *religious* or *nuns*.

Cope (Latin *CAPPA* "cloak with hood") A full-length open cloak, with a rudimentary hood, usually worn over a *cassock* and *surplice* for ceremonies other than *Mass*, such as weddings, *processions* and *Benediction*.

Corporal (Latin *CORPORALE* from *CORPUS*, "body") A square white cloth unfolded on the *altar* to hold the *chalice* and *paten* during *Mass*. It may be stored in a *burse* until it is needed.

Corporal Works of Mercy Seven types of action appropriate for the Christian: feeding the hungry, giving drink to the thirsty, clothing the naked, housing the homeless, visiting the sick, visiting the imprisoned, burying the dead. See also *Spiritual Works of Mercy*.

Corpus Christi (Latin, "Body of Christ") The Thursday after *Trinity Sunday*, a *Solemnity* to celebrate the gift of the *Eucharist*, marked with *processions* and solemn *Benediction*; now, in England and Wales, celebrated on the nearest Sunday.

Cotta (Italian, "cut short") A shortened form of the *surplice*, worn over a *cassock* by those serving *Mass*.

Council A meeting of *bishops* to discuss matters of Christian *doctrine*, morals and discipline. Councils may be local, consisting of bishops from a particular nation or region, sometimes called a *Synod*, or they may involve all the bishops of the world in a **General Council**, also called an **Ecumenical Council** (Greek *OIKOUMENÉ*, "inhabited world"). The doctrinal decisions of a General Council may be formally defined and thus become part of the *Deposit of Faith*; pastoral and disciplinary decisions may be changed later.

Credence Table (often simply **Credence**) (French *CREDENCE*, Italian *CREDENZA* "sideboard") A small table used for the *sacred vessels* before they are placed on the *altar at Mass*.

Creed (Latin *CREDO*, "I believe") A text setting out the articles of Catholic faith; the best-known are the **Apostles' Creed**, used at *Baptism*, and the **Nicene Creed**, often used at *Mass* on Sundays. The much longer **Athanasian Creed** is encountered only rarely.

Crosier (two words, French *CROISIER* "cross-bearer" and Old French *CROCIER* "bearer of a bishop's crook" here are combined, and their sense transferred from the bearer of the object to the object itself) A long staff of metal or wood, topped with a curled head like a shepherd's crook, carried by *bishops* and *abbots* as a symbol of their pastoral care. Some times called a *pastoral staff* or a crook.

Cross (i) The primary symbol of the Christian faith, representing the cross on which Jesus died; (ii) a term for the salutary suffering given by God to the individual Christian to lead him to holiness. See *Sign of the Cross*.

Crucifix A *cross* bearing the figure of Jesus crucified (the figure is sometimes called a **Corpus**).

Cruets Small glass or metal jugs to contain wine and water for use at *Mass*.

Curate (Latin *CURATUS* "one with responsibility for the care of souls") Used in English to mean a junior or assistant *priest*. In France, a curé is a *parish priest*.

Curia (Latin, "court") (i) Generally, any administrative organisation helping a *bishop* govern a *diocese*; (ii) with the definite article, and sometimes capitalized, the administrative offices of the *Holy See*.

CWL See *Catholic Womens' League*.

Czestochowa Shrine of *Our Lady* in Poland, home of a famous icon (**Our Lady of Czestochowa**).

D

Dalmatic (Latin [*VESTIS* or *TUNICA*] *DALMATICA*, "Balkan-style garment") A three-quarter length closed garment with short wide sleeves, matching the *chasuble*, worn by the *deacon* at *Mass*. Also worn by the *bishop* under his *chasuble* on solemn occasions.

Deacon (Greek *DIAKONOS*, "servant") A man ordained to serve and assist the *Church*. Now often divided into **permanent deacons** (older men, often married, who remain deacons) and transitional deacons, who later proceed to *ordination* as *priests*.

Dean (Latin *DECANUS* "controller of ten") A *priest* chosen to serve a group of priests, either living in community or at least nominally so: the dean of a *cathedral* or of a *chapter* is responsible for the *canons*; and the dean of a **deanery** (in America called a *Vicar Forane*) cares for a subdivision of a *diocese*, usually about ten parishes.

Decalogue (Greek *DEKALOGIA* "ten sayings") See *Commandments, Ten*.

Deposit of Faith The body of teaching, entrusted to us through the *Church* of past ages, which develops and grows as the Church does. See *Tradition*.

Devil's Advocate See *Promoter of the Faith*.

Dicastery (Greek *DIKASTERION*, "place where justice is done") General term for any department of the administration of the *Holy See*.

Diocese (Late Latin *DIOCESIS* "district, governor's jurisdiction"; Greek *DIOIKESIS* "administration, government, province" from *DIOIKEIN* "keep house, administer") An area of territory administered for *Church* purposes by a *bishop*, possessing a *cathedral*. The diocese was an administrative region of the late Roman Empire which survived in the Church long after the Empire had fallen. Adj., **Diocesan**.

Disciple (Latin *DISCIPULUS* "pupil, one who is taught") Often found in *Scripture* as a general term for the followers of Jesus, including the *Apostles*.

Discipline A small whip of cord, once used as means of voluntary *penance*.

Dismissal The concluding part of *Mass* when the congregation is sent out to the world.

Divine Mercy A devotion celebrating the love and mercy of God, often made on the Sunday after *Easter* (**Divine Mercy Sunday**); originating in Poland.

Divine Office The round of prayers for different times of the day used by *monks*, *nuns*, and *priests*, and often by *lay people* as well; well known elements being *Matins*, *Lauds*, *Vespers* and *Compline*. The Office used also to include the so-called *Little Hours* (*Prime*, *Terce*, *Sext*, *None*) now subsumed into *Prayer during the Day* (also called *Midday Prayer*). See also *breviary*.

Divine Praises A series of short invocations of God and the *saints*, commonly repeated after *Benediction*.

Doctor of the Church (Latin *DOCTOR*, "teacher") A *saint* whose learning and writings have made a significant contribution to the development of Christian *doctrine*.

Doctrine (Latin, *DOCTRINA* "teaching" from *DOCERE* "to teach") Truth taught by the *Church* as necessary to be believed by the faithful; this can be either revealed truth (*dogma*), the conclusions of theological reasoning, or part of the natural law.

Dogma (Greek, "opinion, belief" from *DOKEIN*, "to think, suppose") A statement of the *Church's* belief, proposed as something to be held definitively by all Christians as formally revealed by God. Study of dogma is often called **Dogmatic Theology**. See *heresy*.

Dolour Rosary A *chaplet* used for meditating on the *Seven Sorrows of Mary*.

Dominicans Members of a large family of *friars* and *nuns* inspired by the example of St Dominic, with a particular mission to preach and write. In England known as *Blackfriars* because they wear black outer cloaks.

Doxology (Greek *DOXA* "glory" and *LOGIA* "discourse") A prayer or formula giving glory to God; often used to conclude other prayers (the *Eucharistic Prayer* and each decade of the *Rosary* end with doxologies).

E

Easter The greatest feast in the Christian calendar, the *Passover* of the Lord, marking the death and resurrection of Jesus and his winning for us victory over sin and death, and the gift of eternal life. Celebrations begin with the *Triduum* at the end of *Holy Week*, marking the end of the forty days of *Lent* and the beginning of the fifty days of **Eastertide** until *Pentecost*. In the northern hemisphere, **Easter Sunday** is celebrated on the first Sunday after the first full moon of spring. See also *Pasch*.

Easter Duties Every Catholic is obliged to go to *Confession* and receive *Holy Communion* at least once a year (see *Commandments of the Church*); traditionally this was done during *Lent* or *Eastertide*, and hence is known as making one's Easter Duties.

Easter Vigil A *liturgy* of prayer, *Scripture* and singing during the night before *Easter Sunday*, including the blessing of the *Paschal Candle*, celebration of *Baptism*, and ending with the *Eucharist*. The Easter Vigil is the culmination of the *Triduum*, opening the **Season of Easter**. In the early Church, it was celebrated during the night, ending with the Eucharist at dawn. After the liturgical renewal following the Second Vatican Council, the Church has encouraged the recovery of this way of celebrating the Easter Vigil.

Easter Week From *Easter Sunday* to *Low Sunday*.

Ecclesiology That branch of theology dealing with the nature of the *Church*.

Ecumenical Council See *Council*.

Ecumenism, earlier **Œcumenism** (Greek *OIKOUMENÉ*, "inhabited world") The movement which began in earnest after the Second Vatican Council, attempting to bring all Christians, Catholic and non-Catholic, into closer unity.

Election, Rite of A ceremony to welcome *catechumens* who are in the last stages of preparation for *Baptism*, sometimes celebrated publicly before the *bishop* during *Lent*.

Ember Days (Old English *YMBRENDAGAS*, etymology obscure, perhaps from Old English *YMBRENE*, "period of time", or a corruption of Latin *QUATTUOR TEMPORA* "four times") Formerly, days on which *fasting* and *abstinence* were obligatory for all Catholics, associated with seasonal times of sowing and harvest. They were the Wednesdays, Fridays and Saturdays of the weeks following the Third Sunday of *Advent*, the First Sunday of *Lent*, *Pentecost*, and the seventeenth Sunday after *Pentecost*. Now replaced by days of special prayer and fasting as determined by local *bishops*. See *Rogation Days*.

Embolism (Greek *EMBOLISMOS* "something stuck in or intercalated" from *EMBALLEIN* "to throw in") Generally, any prayer inserted into another, or amplifying it; usually refers to the prayer at *Mass* after the *Our Father*, which develops the last petition of that prayer.

Encyclical (Latin *ENCYCLICUS* from Greek *ENKUKLIOS*, from *ENKUKLO* "in a circle") A circular letter from the *Pope* addressed to the whole world, setting out some important teaching often at some length. Usually known by the first two words of its text in Latin.

Epiclesis (Greek, "calling down, invocation" from *EPIKALEO*, "to invoke") That part of a *Eucharistic Prayer* in which the *Holy Spirit* is invoked to come down on the offerings of bread and wine to transform them.

Epiphany (Greek *EPI-PHANEIA*, "a making manifest") The *Solemnity* on 6th January commemorating the manifestation of Jesus to the world: at the visit of the Magi, his Baptism in the Jordan, and the marriage at Cana. Formerly called **Twelfth Night** (after Christmas). In the older liturgical calendar, followed by the **Season of Epiphany** meditating on these themes until just before *Lent*.

Epistle (Latin *EPISTOLA* "letter") Traditional name for the first reading at *Mass*, which usually came from an Epistle (letter) of St Paul; traditionally read from the right hand side of the *altar*, as the people see it.

Eschatology (Greek *ESCHATALOGIA*, from *ESCHATA* "the last things" and *LOGIA* "discourse") Theological reflection on God's final destiny for his creation. See *Second Coming*, *Parousia*.

Eucharist (Greek, *EUKHARISTIA*, "giving thanks") (i) Primarily, the *Mass*, the sacrament of the Body and Blood of Jesus Christ under the form of bread and wine, consecrated by a *priest* who represents Christ to his *Church*. Receiving *Holy Communion* at Mass allows the Christian faithful truly to become the Body of Christ, the Church. (ii) the consecrated elements, the *Blessed Sacrament*.

Eucharistic Adoration Worship of the reserved *Blessed Sacrament*.

Eucharistic Congress A national or international gathering to reflect on the *Eucharist*.

Eucharistic Fast The obligation on all Catholics who have made their *First Communion*, under sixty years of age and in good health, to abstain from food and drink for an hour before receiving *Holy Communion*. A *priest* must fast for an hour before the start of *Mass*. Water or medicine does not break the fast. Formerly fasting was obligatory from the previous midnight.

Eucharistic Minister A widely used, but incorrect term for an *Extraordinary Minister of Holy Communion* (also, again incorrectly, often called a *Special Minister*).

Eucharistic Prayer The central prayer of the Mass, incorporating an *Epiclesis* and the *Consecration*. See *Canon*, *Anaphora*.

Evangelical Counsels Voluntary poverty, chastity and obedience.

Evangelization (Latin *EVANGELIZO*, Greek *EVANGELIZOMAI* "bring good news") The process of introducing people to the truths of the *Gospel*, an essential part of *mission*.

Evening Prayer An alternative name for *Vespers*.

Examination of Conscience A brief review of one's life and actions to identify one's sins. It should be made before *confession*, and may be made daily.

Excommunication Formal recognition that a person has by his actions or beliefs separated himself from the *Church*, the Body of Christ, and is thus unable to approach the *sacraments*.

Exorcist (Latin *EXORCISTA*, from Greek *EX ORKIZO*, "adjure") Originally the third grade of *Holy Orders*, now suspended in the Latin Church. The ministry of **Exorcism**, delivering people or places from malign or demonic influences, is now entrusted only to a senior *priest* of notable common sense and stability.

Exposition (of the Blessed Sacrament) Placing the consecrated *Host* in a *monstrance* and displaying it for *adoration*.

Exsultet (Latin, "Let [the choir of angels] rejoice") Ancient hymn opening the *Easter Vigil*; also called the *Paschal Praeconium*.

Extraordinary Form The older form of the Roman Rite, according to the edition of 1962 (the last published before the reforms of the Second Vatican Council). See also *Tridentine Rite*, *Mass of John XXIII*.

Extraordinary Minister of Holy Communion A person, often one of the *laity*, appointed to assist with the distribution of *Holy Communion* at *Mass* in cases of necessity where the number of *priests* or *deacons* present is insufficient, or to take Communion to the sick or housebound. Often incorrectly called a *Special Minister* or *Eucharistic Minister*.

F

Faculty Formal permission, usually in writing, from a *bishop* allowing a *priest* to exercise his ministry (by celebrating the *sacraments* publicly) in a particular *diocese*.

Fascia (Italian, "band, strip") A wide cloth band used to gird the *cassock*, hanging down on the left, often with tassels.

Fast, Eucharistic See *Eucharistic Fast*.

Fasting Self-discipline in matters of food. Traditionally, on a **fast-day** only one meal was permitted, with two light snacks. Although fast-days were once very numerous, including much of *Lent* and *Advent*, Catholics in England and Wales are now obliged to fast only on *Ash Wednesday* and *Good Friday*, which are also days of *abstinence*. Fasting is binding on those in good health over eighteen and under sixty. Many people fast on other days (such as Fridays during Lent) as a voluntary *penance*. See also *Ember Days*, *Rogation Days*.

Fathers of the Church The great writers and preachers who helped form the *Church* particularly during the third, fourth and fifth centuries.

Fátima A village in Portugal, now a major Marian shrine, associated with the apparition of the *Virgin Mary* to three children in 1917; commemorated on 13th May.

Feast-days (informally, **feasts**) The middle rank of special days, between *memorials* and *Solemnities*, for major *saints* and some aspects of the life of Jesus; also used as a general term for all such special days.

Feasts, moveable Certain *feast-days* (*Ash Wednesday*, *Easter*, *Ascension*, *Pentecost*, *Corpus Christi*) the date of whose celebration varies from year to year.

Feria (Latin "holiday") Curiously, in the *Church* an ordinary weekday that is not a holiday, where there is no *saint's* day or other commemoration.

Ferraiuola (also **ferraiuolo** or **ferraiolo**) (Italian) A cloak of light fabric, worn on ceremonial occasions over the *cassock* and *fascia*, usually black, but purple for *prelates* and red for the *Pope*. **Ferraiuolone** or **ferraiolone** is a variant form, sometimes used for a slightly different garment.

Filioque (Latin, "and from the Son") A word added to the Nicene *Creed* in the Western *Church* from the sixth century onwards, expressing the procession of the *Holy Spirit* from the Father and the Son alike. This clarification was not accepted by the Churches of the East (see *Trinity*, *Orthodox Church*).

First Communion, First Holy Communion The first time a baptised Catholic receives *Holy Communion*. In the Western Church this generally occurs at around the age of seven years.

First Fridays A devotion to the *Sacred Heart* consisting in receiving *Communion* on the first Friday of nine consecutive months.

First Saturdays A devotion in honour of the *Virgin Mary* consisting in receiving *Communion* on the first Saturday of five consecutive months.

Focolare (Italian, "hearth") A *new movement* founded in Italy with a particular emphasis on *ecumenism*.

Font (Latin *FONS*, "fountain') A large basin or pool, usually of stone, containing the water used for *baptism*, and sited in the *baptistery* of a *church*.

Footpace The platform in front of an altar for a *priest* to stand during *Mass*.

Forty Hours *Exposition of the Blessed Sacrament* for two and a half days' *adoration*, ending with *Benediction*, usually accompanied by other devotions. Sometimes known by its Italian name, *Quarant' Ore*.

Four Last Things Death, Judgement, Hell and Heaven.

Fraction (Latin *FRACTIO*, "breaking") The breaking of the consecrated *Host* before *Communion* at *Mass*.

Franciscans Members of various orders of *friars* and *nuns* all inspired by the example of St Francis of Assisi, in particular his dedication to "Lady Poverty". Franciscans typically wear a knotted rope around their waists; in England sometimes known as *Greyfriars* although many now wear brown habits.

Friar (Old French *FRÈRE* "brother") A man vowed to religious life as a travelling preacher, under vows of poverty, chastity and obedience, organized in an international *order*; living in a **Friary** but often moving from one to another.

Frontal See *altar*.

Fruits of the Spirit Twelve qualities formed in the Christian by the action of the *Holy Spirit*: charity, joy, peace, patience, kindness, goodness, generosity, gentleness, faithfulness, modesty, self-control, chastity. See *Gifts of the Spirit*.

G

Galera, or "soup-plate hat". A round hat with a broad brim, now rarely seen; *Cardinals* wore red galere with fifteen tassels on each side, other *clergy* varying colours and differing numbers of tassels. Properly worn as street dress.

Gaudete Sunday The third Sunday of *Advent*, when the *introit* begins Gaudete, "rejoice", and the sombre colour of the *vestments* is lightened to rose-pink.

General Absolution Granting *absolution* simultaneously to a number of penitents without preceding individual *confession*. Its use in any cases other than those of extreme necessity (soldiers before battle, for instance) has been forbidden by the *Holy See*. In such cases, receiving it brings an obligation to make an individual confession as soon as is possible.

Genuflect (Latin *GENUFLECTO* "bend the knee") Gesture of respect when passing in front of the *Blessed Sacrament*, kneeling briefly on the right knee. Traditionally if the Blessed Sacrament is *exposed*, one kneels on both knees.

Gifts of the Spirit Seven particular graces (wisdom, understanding, counsel, fortitude, knowledge, piety, the fear of the Lord) given to Christians by the *Holy Spirit* through the *sacraments* of *Baptism* and especially *Confirmation*. See *Fruits of the Spirit*.

Gloria (Latin "glory") A hymn of praise used at *Mass* on *feast-days* and *solemnities* after the *Kyrie*, often set to music.

Glory Be A *doxological* prayer to the *Trinity*, frequently used as part of the *Divine Office* and the *Rosary*.

Godparents Christians who at a *baptism* undertake to support the one being baptized in his Christian life, and (in the case of infant baptism) profess the faith on the child's behalf, and undertake to help the child's parents in their duty to transmit the faith.

Good Friday The Friday before *Easter Sunday*, second day of the *Triduum*, commemorating the triumph of Jesus on the *Cross*. Marked by reading or singing the *Passion*, and veneration of the cross, which both recalls Christ's sacrifice and allows us to accept our own cross.

Gospel (Old English *GŌD SPEL*, "good news") (i) One of the four accounts (known by the names of their authors, Matthew, Mark, Luke and John) of the life and message of Jesus Christ that the *Church* has discerned to be true; (ii) at *Mass*, the reading from one of these Gospels which concludes the *Liturgy of the Word*; (iii) the content of the Church's *preaching* and *evangelization*, namely Christ's life and teaching as expressed in the Gospels and *New Testament* letters.

Grace The action or presence of God in the Christian life; a particular manifestation of this in the experience of the Christian.

Grace before Meals A prayer of thanksgiving before eating.

Gradine (Italian *GRADINO* "little step" from *GRADO* "step") A step or shelf running along the back of an *altar* set against the wall, which may serve to hold candles, flowers or *reliquaries*.

Gradual A *psalm* text after the first reading at *Mass*, formerly sung to a slow chant; now typically known as the *responsorial psalm*, and sung *antiphonally*. Hence **Graduale**, a book containing chants for the gradual and other parts of the Mass.

Great O Antiphons During the last week before *Christmas*, the *Magnificat* at *Vespers* is introduced with particularly elaborate *antiphons*, each one beginning with O; the last is "O Emmanuel". The hymn "O come, O come, Emmanuel" translates them.

Greyfriars Traditional English name for *Franciscans*.

Guadalupe A village in Mexico, now a Marian shrine associated with the apparition of the *Virgin Mary* to Juan Diego in 1531 commemorated on 13th December. **Our Lady of Guadalupe**, the miraculous image given to Juan Diego, is also a title of the *Virgin Mary* as *patron* of the Americas and of unborn children.

H

Habit (Latin *HABITUS*, "costume") The distinctive garb of a member of a *religious order*.

Hail Holy Queen A prayer to the *Virgin Mary* dating from the eleventh century, often said to conclude the *Rosary* and at the end of *Compline*. See *Salve Regina*.

Hail Mary The most popular prayer to the *Virgin Mary*, composed mainly of words from *Scripture*. See *Ave Maria*.

Hand Missal See *Missal*.

Heresy (Greek *HAIRESIS*, from *HAIREIN* "to choose") An erroneous belief, knowingly and deliberately held, about an essential Christian truth. Strictly, a heresy is a conscious and deliberate denial of a *dogma* of the *Church* by one who still claims to be a Catholic. One who publicly and repeatedly affirms a heresy is called a **heretic**, and is subject to *excommunication*.

Hermits (Greek *EREMITA*, from *ERÉMIA* "desert" or *EREMOS* "solitary") Those who live a life dedicated to prayer on their own. May be grouped into communities with some degree of common life, like *Carthusians* and *Camaldolese*.

Hierarchy (Greek *HIERARKHIA*, "the high priests") The organised body of *bishops* entrusted with the task of governing the *Church*.

High Altar Old name for the main *altar* in a large *church*.

High Mass *Mass* in the *Extraordinary Form* sung by a *priest* with the assistance of a *deacon* and *sub-deacon* (usually both also priests) with, often, a choir. When sung by a priest alone, with or without a choir, it is known as a **Missa Cantata**. These distinctions do not apply to *Mass* in the *Ordinary Form* of the Roman Rite. See also *Low Mass*.

Hilary Term The spring term at older English universities, so called because it begins at around the time of St Hilary's *feast-day* (January 13th).

Holy Communion See *Communion, Holy*.

Holy Days of Obligation Solemn *feasts* of the *Church* falling on weekdays when all Catholics are obliged to attend *Mass* just as they do on a Sunday and, in theory at least, to abstain from work. A number of these are celebrated by all Catholics everywhere; others apply only in particular countries. The full list of universal Holy Days contains four feasts of *Our Lord*: *Christmas* (25th December), *Epiphany* (6th January), *Ascension* (forty days after Easter), *Corpus Christi* (the Thursday after *Trinity Sunday*); three of *Our Lady*: the *Mother of God* (1st January), the *Assumption* (15th August), and the *Immaculate Conception* (8th December); and three celebrating the *saints*: *St Joseph* (19th March), *SS Peter and Paul* (29th June), and *All Saints* (1st November). In England and Wales a number of these *solemnities* are not observed, or have been transferred to the nearest Sunday; those that are still observed on weekdays are Christmas, the Assumption, SS Peter and Paul, and All Saints.

Holy Family The earthly family of Jesus; usually understood as comprising Jesus, Mary and Joseph, but can be extended to all the cousins mentioned in *Scripture*. The Sunday after *Christmas* is the feast-day of the Holy Family.

Holy Ghost (Old English *GAST*, "spirit") Older English name for the *Holy Spirit*.

Holy Holy Holy See *Sanctus*.

Holy Hour A ceremony of exposition of the *Blessed Sacrament* for one hour's *adoration*, ending with *Benediction*.

Holy Name The name of Jesus, the name through which we are saved; the *Feast* of the Holy Name is on 3rd January.

Holy Office Old name for the *Congregation of the Doctrine of the Faith* (CDF).

Holy Saturday The day before *Easter Sunday*, within the *Triduum*, marked by quiet expectation and austerity, when no *Mass* or *sacraments* are celebrated, in anticipation of the *Easter Vigil*.

Holy See The *Papacy*. A bishop's see (from the Latin *SEDES*, "seat") refers both to the *diocese* he governs and to his authority over it. The *Pope*, as Bishop of Rome, occupies the See of Rome, which has primacy over all other Christian churches; it is traditionally called the Holy See to mark this. This term can also refer to the various administrative offices (or *dicasteries*) which assist the Pope in different ways. See also *Vatican*.

Holy Souls The souls of the dead in *Purgatory*; see *All Souls*.

Holy Spirit The third Person of the *Trinity*, often represented by a dove.

Holy Water Blessed water used as a *sacramental*.

Holy Week The last week of *Lent*, beginning with *Palm* (or *Passion*) *Sunday* a week before *Easter Sunday*, and culminating in the *Triduum*; spent contemplating and preparing to celebrate the Easter *mysteries*: the passion, death, and resurrection of Jesus.

Homily (Greek *HOMILO* "speak") A discourse in which the *priest* explains the readings at *Mass*; also called a *sermon*.

Hosanna (late Latin form of Hebrew *HŌSHA'NĀ* "save, we pray!") A Jewish liturgical formula taken over into the Christian *liturgy*.

Host (Latin *HOSTIA* "sacrificial victim") The consecrated *Eucharist* in the form of bread; the large host is broken by the *priest* at *Mass*, and small hosts are used to distribute to the people, and to reserve in the *Tabernacle*. Also used casually to mean unconsecrated *altar-breads*.

Humeral veil (Latin *HUMERALIS* from *(H)UMERUS*, "upper arm, shoulder") A broad band of fabric placed around the shoulders of a *priest* or *deacon* who is carrying the *Blessed Sacrament*, or when giving the blessing at *Benediction*.

I

ICEL Abbreviation for the **International Commission on English in the Liturgy**, the official body entrusted with translating the *Church's liturgy* into English.

IHS The first three letters of "Jesus" in Greek capitals, often used as a monogram. Sometimes interpreted as an abbreviation of Iesus Hominum Salvator ("Jesus, Saviour of Men") or In Hoc Signo ("in this sign [of the cross, you shall conquer]").

Immaculate Conception The doctrine that the *Virgin Mary* was "chosen before creation began", and prepared by God to be the Mother of Christ, preserved free from *Original Sin*, and thus able to make a free choice to co-operate with God. Celebrated on 8th December with a *Solemnity*. To be distinguished from the *Virgin Birth*.

Immaculate Heart The heart of the *Virgin Mary*, a model for us, totally dedicated to the will of God. The *feast* of the Immaculate Heart of Mary is celebrated on the Saturday after the second Sunday after *Pentecost*, the day following the feast of the *Sacred Heart* of Jesus.

Imprimatur (Latin, "let it be printed") An official declaration by a *bishop* that a book or similar document accords with the teaching of the *Church*. See also *Nihil Obstat*.

Incardination (Latin *INCARDINATIO* from *INCARDINO* "attach [to a particular church] like a hinge to a door": see *Cardinal*) The act whereby a *cleric* is incorporated into a particular *diocese* or religious *order*.

Incarnation (Latin, *INCARNATIO* from *INCARNARE* "to become flesh" from *CARO* "flesh, body") The coming to birth as man of God the Son, the Second Person of the *Holy Trinity*, as Jesus of Nazareth, the *Christ*.

Incense Grains of consolidated gum which give off scented smoke when burnt. Used at *Mass* and other ceremonies, to represent the prayers of the *saints* rising up to heaven (see *Ps* 140 v.2). Kept in an **incense-boat**, and ladled out with an **incense-spoon** onto glowing charcoal in a *thurible* or *censer*.

Index Shortened form of the **Index Librorum Prohibitorum** (Latin, "list of forbidden books") a list of books judged to be dangerous to faith and morals and thus only to be read by Catholics with special permission from the *Holy See*. First compiled in 1557 and abolished in 1966.

Indulgence, either **partial** or **plenary** A papal grant and gift of *grace* remitting part or all of the temporal punishment due for one's sins; attached conditions will include the *sacraments* and *prayer*, and a firm purpose to amend one's life. Can be gained for oneself or for the *Holy Souls* in *Purgatory*.

Indult (Latin *INDULTUM* "something allowed for") A letter from the Pope giving permission for a particular *Canon Law* to be suspended in particular circumstances.

Infallibility The *dogma* that the *Church's* teaching on faith or morals is divinely guaranteed against being mistaken. It applies both to the consensus teaching of the Church (the "ordinary *Magisterium*") and to solemn pronouncements by the *Pope* speaking on behalf of all the Church's *bishops*.

Infant of Prague (also called the *Child of Prague*) An image of the child Jesus wearing very elaborate robes and crown. The original is in the *Carmelite* church in Prague (given to them in 1628).

Infulae (Latin "bands, fillets") The streamers hanging from a *mitre*.

Inquisition (Latin *INQUISITIO* "enquiry") The Roman Inquisition (a body quite distinct, unexpectedly, from the Spanish Inquisition) was later renamed the *Holy Office*, and is now the *Congregation of the Doctrine of the Faith*.

INRI Abbreviation of Iesus Nazarenus Rex Iudaeorum (Latin, "Jesus of Nazareth King of the Jews"), the inscription affixed by Pilate to the cross.

Introit (Latin *INTROITUS*, "entry") The first *proper* text of the *Mass*: a verse of *Scripture* to set the theme. The first word of the introit is often used to designate the whole Mass, e.g. *Requiem*.

J

James, Liturgy of Saint One of the three Eucharistic liturgies commonly used by the *Orthodox Church*.

Jesuits Popular name for the *Society of Jesus*, an *order* of *priests* founded by St Ignatius of Loyola in the sixteenth century. They take a special *vow*, in addition to the usual ones of *poverty*, *chastity* and *obedience*, to put themselves absolutely at the disposal of the *Pope* for the purposes of *mission*. Historically very active in education at all levels; more recently often associated with practical, and sometimes controversial, implementation of the *Church's* social teaching.

Jesus Prayer A devotion, originating in the *Orthodox Church*, usually using a *chaplet* or a prayer-rope, on each bead or knot of which are said the words "Lord Jesus Christ Son of God have mercy on me a sinner" or variants thereon.

K

Kerygma (Greek, "proclamation") The announcement of the saving message of the *Gospel*.

Knights of Columbus An American association of laymen, founded in New Haven Connecticut in 1882, analogous to the *Knights of St Columba.*

Knights of the Holy Sepulchre In full, the Equestrian Order of the Holy Sepulchre of Jerusalem, originally constituted in the fifteenth century to protect Christians in the Holy Land. Membership is now a purely honorific distinction conferred by the *Holy See.*

Knights of Malta In full, the Sovereign Military Hospitaller Order of St John of Jerusalem, of Rhodes and of Malta, sometimes called the Knights Hospitaller. Originally a military organization, founded in 1070 to defend Christendom against Islamic aggression; now primarily involved in charitable work. It is formally constituted as an independent sovereign state under a Grand Master.

Knights of St Columba An association of men devoted to *evangelization* and practical works of charity.

Kyrie (Greek, "O Lord") A repetitive chant asking for mercy, near the beginning of *Mass*, and often set to music.

L

Lady Chapel In most Catholic *churches*, a subsidiary *altar* (usually on the north side, to the right of the *high altar*) dedicated to the *Blessed Virgin Mary*.

Lady Day A traditional English name for the *Annunciation*.

Laetare Sunday The fourth Sunday of *Lent*, when the introit begins Laetare, "rejoice", and the sombre colour of the vestments is lightened to a rose-pink.

Laity (Greek *LAIKOS* from *LAOS* "people") Also called **lay people**: those members of the Church, the majority, not set aside as *clergy* or *religious*.

Lamb of God See *Agnus Dei*.

Lammas (Old English *HLĀFMÆSSE* "festival of bread") Traditional name for the feast of St Peter in Chains (August 1st) kept as a harvest festival.

Last Blessing Traditional term for the blessing given by the *priest* near the end of *Mass*.

Last Gospel The opening verses of St John's *Gospel*, read at the end of the Traditional Latin (*Tridentine*) Mass.

Last Rites Historically, the *sacrament* of *anointing* given to those near death. No longer an accurate description of the Anointing of the Sick, or the *Last Sacraments*. See also *Extreme Unction*.

Last Sacraments For those about to die, the *priest* if possible administers the *Sacrament of Penance*, with *absolution* and a Plenary *Indulgence*, and *Holy Communion* (*viaticum*). If the sick person has not yet been *anointed*, that may be done too.

Lateran The *Basilica* of St John in Lateran is the official seat of the *Pope* as Bishop of Rome, and was his residence until the fifteenth century.

Lauds (Latin *LAUDES*, "praises") The second hour of the *Divine Office*, also known as *Morning Prayer*; it contains *psalms* including those of praise, and the *Benedictus* or Canticle of Zechariah.

Lavabo (Latin "I will wash") The stage at *Mass* when the *priest* washes his hands, so-called because in the older (*Tridentine*) rite of Mass verses 6-12 of Psalm 25 which open with this word are then said; hence the **lavabo-basin** and the **lavabo-towel** for the priest's use.

Lay Apostolate The role of the *laity* in spreading the faith, consisting in *evangelization* and *almsgiving*, nourished by prayer and study.

Lay people See *laity*.

Lectern (Medieval Latin *LECTRINUM*) A stand to hold the book from which *Scripture* is read at *Mass*, or Scripture and the writings of the *Church Fathers* at *Matins*. May be decorated with a fabric *lectern-fall* to match the *vestments*. See *Ambo*.

Lectio Divina (Latin, "sacred reading") Slow prayerful reading, usually of *Scripture*, originally practised in *monasteries*.

Lectionary (Latin *LECTIONARIUM*, from *LECTIO*, "reading") The book containing the readings from the Bible used at *Mass*.

Lector (Latin, "reader") Originally the second grade of *Holy Orders*, now suspended in the Latin Church. Now used for a lay ministry, assistant to the *priest*, hardly ever conferred except for those on the way to *ordination* as *deacon* or *priest*. Also used informally for those who proclaim the Word of God (reading) in the *liturgy*, usually at *Mass*.

Legilium (neo-Latin) A folding portable *lectern*.

Legion of Christ An order of *clergy* devoted to *evangelization*.

Legion of Mary An association of *lay people* devoted to *evangelization*.

Lent (Old English *LENCTEN*, "spring") The season of *penance* from *Ash Wednesday* to *Easter Sunday*, consisting of forty days.

Liber Cantualis (Latin, "Book of Chant") A collection of simple *Gregorian chant* settings of liturgical texts published by the Abbey of Solesmes in France.

Liber Usualis (Latin, "Customary Book") A comprehensive book containing *Gregorian chant* settings for the *Mass* and the *Divine Office*, published by the French Abbey of Solesmes.

Limbo (ablative form of Latin *LIMBUS*, "border, fringe") Historically, the supposed destination of children who died unbaptized, and of the righteous who lived before Christ: a place of natural happiness but lacking the fullness of *beatitude*. Recent discernment by the *Magisterium* has judged the notion to be superfluous.

Litany (Greek *LITANEIA* "prayer") A prayer consisting of many short invocations with a common response, often used at *Benediction* or during *Exposition*. The most popular is the **Litany of Loreto**, a litany invoking the prayers of the *Virgin Mary*. The **Litany of the Saints** is used at *Ordinations* and often at *Baptisms*.

Little Hours The four hours of the *Divine Office* in the daytime, *Prime*, *Terce*, *Sext* and *None*; now, after the liturgical reforms of the Second Vatican Council, subsumed into *Prayer during the Day*. See *Divine Office*.

Little Office A short round of daily prayers to the *Virgin Mary* after the model of the full *Divine Office*, sometimes said instead of, or in addition to, that Office.

Liturgy (Greek *LEITOURGIA*, "public service, worship") The public worship of the *Church* in general; in particular the *Mass* and the *Divine Office*. Hence the **Liturgy of the Word**, the first half of the *Mass* featuring the *Scripture* readings; and **Liturgy of the Eucharist**, the second half, with the *Eucharistic Prayer* and *Communion*. The **Liturgy of the Hours** is another name for the *Divine Office*.

Lord's Day Sunday.

Lord's Prayer The *Our Father*.

Lourdes French Pyrenean village, now a major Marian shrine associated with the apparitions of the *Virgin Mary* to Bernadette Soubirous in 1858. The first apparition is commemorated on 11th February, the *feast-day* of Our Lady of Lourdes.

Low Mass *Mass* in the *Extraordinary Form* of the Roman Rite, spoken not sung.

Low Sunday Traditional English name for the Sunday after *Easter*, sometimes called *Quasimodo Sunday* (after the first word of the Latin *introit* for the *Mass* of the day). The exact origin of the term "Low Sunday" is obscure; as it is the *octave* day of Easter, it may originally have been an analogy from the eight note musical scale (where Easter Sunday is the first note). Now also known as *Divine Mercy Sunday*.

Lucernarium (Latin, "service of lamps" from *LUCERNA* "lamp") Originally, a name for solemn *Vespers* celebrated at a *cathedral*; now often used for any liturgical ceremony involving new light, such as that which opens the *Easter Vigil*.

M

Madonna (Italian, "my Lady") The *Virgin Mary*.

Magisterium (neo-Latin, from *MAGISTER*, "master, teacher") The teaching authority of the *Church*, specifically the *Pope* with his assistants, and *General Councils*.

Magnificat (Latin, "[My soul] magnifies [the Lord]") The *canticle* of Mary (*Lk* 1:46-55), used at *Vespers*.

Maniple (Latin *MANIPULUS* "handful") The fourth of the *vestments* for *Mass*, a band of fabric matching the *stole*, worn over the left arm, but now usually omitted. Originally used as a handkerchief, subsequently purely symbolic in function.

Mantilla (Spanish "mantle, headscarf") A lace head-covering, originally a Spanish fashion, often worn in church by women of a traditionalist cast in response to St Paul's injunction (1 *Co* 11:5-6)

Martinmas Traditional English name for the feast of the Translation of St Martin of Tours (11th November).

Martyr (Greek *MARTUR*, *MARTUS*, "witness") One who gives witness to the faith by accepting death. To be a martyr the person must be confronted with a real choice over whether to abandon the faith or remain loyal and be killed.

Martyrology (Latin *MARTYROLOGIUM*, Greek *MARTUROLOGION* "book of witnesses") A calendar listing, for each day of the year, all the *saints* whose *feast-days* are celebrated on that day; the **Roman Martyrology** is the official such list for the universal *Church*.

Mass (Latin *MISSA*, "sending, dismissal") The central act of Christian worship, in which, after *Scripture* is proclaimed and prayers are made, the *priest* consecrates the bread and wine to become the *Eucharist*.

Mass of Blessed John XXIII See *Extraordinary Form*.

Mass of Paul VI Another name for the revised rite of *Mass* promulgated by Pope Paul VI in 1969. See *Ordinary Form*, *Novus Ordo*, *Tridentine Rite*, *Extraordinary Form*.

Mass of the Catechumens Old term for the first half of *Mass*, everything up to the *Gospel* and *homily*; so called because in the early *Church* the unbaptized under instruction (*catechumens*) were allowed to be present during this part of the *liturgy*.

Mass of the Faithful Old term for the second half of *Mass*, principally the *Eucharistic Prayer* and *Holy Communion*. So called because in the early Church *catechumens* (unbaptized people under instruction) were not permitted to be present for this part of the Mass, which was reserved for the baptized (the faithful) alone.

Mass of the Presanctified A *Mass* where the *Eucharistic Prayer* is not said, and *Communion* is distributed using *Hosts* previously consecrated; historically often used to describe the *liturgy* on *Good Friday*.

Matins (Latin *MATUTINA*, "morning") Sometimes known as *Vigils* or the *Office of Readings*, the first and longest hour of the *Divine Office*, containing *psalms* and long readings from *Scripture* and the *Fathers of the Church*. Traditionally celebrated during the night. The spelling "Mattins" is generally used by Anglicans.

Matrimony The holy *sacrament* of marriage by which one man and one woman are joined in lifelong faithfulness, a living icon of the union between Christ and His *Church*.

Maundy Thursday (Old French *MANDÉ*, Latin *MANDATUM*, "commandment') The Thursday of *Holy Week*, the first day of the *Triduum*, on which is celebrated the New Commandment to love one another (*Jn* 13-17), as expressed by Jesus's washing the feet of the *Apostles*; and the Last Supper, the institution of the *Eucharist*.

Meditation Mental *prayer* using intellect and reason to ponder on some text of *Scripture* or point of *doctrine*, and draw conclusions.

Memorare (Latin, "Remember [O most gracious Virgin Mary]") A medieval prayer to the *Virgin Mary*, attributed to St Bernard of Clairvaux (ob.1153)

Memorial The lowest rank of *feast-days*, for minor *saints* and those of local interest only; some Memorials are optional, others compulsory.

Metropolitan (Greek *MÉTÉR*, "mother" and *POLIS*, "city") Alternative name for an *Archbishop*, whose seat may be called a **Metropolitan Cathedral**.

Michaelmas Traditional English name for the feast of St Michael the Archangel (September 29th); at older English universities, the autumn term, which typically began at around that time.

Midday Prayer, also called *Prayer during the Day*. Short hour of the *Divine Office* celebrated during the day; in the reformed *Breviary*, this single *liturgy* replaces the old canonical hours of *Prime*, *Terce*, *Sext* and *None*.

Mid-Lent Sunday See *Laetare Sunday*.

Miraculous Medal A particular design of medal, bearing an image of the *Virgin Mary* under the aspect of the *Immaculate Conception*, used as a *sacramental*. The design was revealed to St Catherine Labouré in 1830.

Miserere (Latin, "have mercy") In the *Vulgate* bible, the opening word of Psalm 51, one of the *penitential psalms*; used as an abbreviation for that Psalm.

Missa Cantata See *High Mass*.

Missal A book containing all the texts of the *Mass*. These include the *Ordinary of the Mass* (also called the *Order of Mass*) which consists of the unchanging parts (including the *Eucharistic Prayers*); the prayers (*introits*, *collects*, *offertory prayers*, *prefaces*, *post-communion* prayers) for different Sundays and *feast-days* (these are sometimes called *Propers*); and the Bible readings for Sundays and feast-days taken from the *Lectionary*. Many Catholics will own a small Missal (sometimes called a *hand Missal*) for use at Mass. *Priests* saying Mass will often use a Missal without the Lectionary readings; this is known as an *Altar Missal* or *Sacramentary*.

Mission (Latin *MISSIO*, "sending") (i) The responsibility of every Christian to bring the Word of God into the world; (ii) a location from which **missionaries** (*clergy, religious* and *laity*) can begin the work of spreading the Word of God. Once well-established, a mission will become a *parish*.

Missionaries of Charity An *order* of *nuns* founded by Blessed Teresa of Calcutta (Mother Teresa) to work amongst the poor and dying, originally in India but now also worldwide.

Mitre (Greek *MITRA* "turban, headband, hat") The distinctive headdress of a *bishop*, rising to a peak in front and behind, with two streamers or *infulae* hanging down behind.

Mixed Marriage Broadly considered, marriage between a Catholic and a non-Catholic; usually refers to marriage between a Catholic and a baptized non-Catholic Christian.

Monastery (Greek *MONASTÉRION* from *MONAZEIN*, "live alone", *MONOS*, "solitary") The home of a community of vowed *monks* or *nuns*.

Monk (Old English *MUNUC* from Latin *MONACHUS*, Greek *MONAKHOS* from *MONOS*, "solitary") A man who dedicates his life to prayer, taking *vows* to remain in the same place for life, under *obedience*, and living as befits a monk, that is without owning anything as an individual (poverty) and in continence (chastity).

Monsignor (Italian *MON SIGNORE*, French MON *SEIGNEUR*, "my lord, my superior") Courtesy title for various grades of *prelate*; in England used only for those below the rank of *bishop*.

Monstrance (Latin *MONSTRANTIA* "a showing", from *MONSTRARE* "to show") A stand, usually shaped like a rayed sun, to contain and display the *Blessed Sacrament* during *Benediction* and *Exposition.*

Morning Prayer An alternative name for *Lauds.*

Mortal Sin (Latin *MORTALIS* "deadly") A serious violation of the law of God; it must be freely chosen, be an act that is objectively gravely wrong, and the person committing it must be aware that it is gravely wrong. Such a sin "kills the soul" and must be repented of in *confession* before one approaches *Communion.* See *venial sin.*

Mortification (Latin *MORTIFICATIO* "making die, putting to death") The spiritual discipline of "dying to self" to make space for God; any ascetical practice designed to promote this.

Mother of God A *Solemnity* on January 1st in honour of Mary, mother of Jesus (formerly the feast of the *Circumcision*). See *Theotokos.*

Motu Proprio (Latin "on his own initiative") A letter from the *Pope* making a decision on some minor matter.

Mozzetta (Italian, "something cut short") A shoulder cape, often fur-lined, worn by senior *clergy* (*canons* and above). See *almuce.*

Mystery (Greek *MUSTERION*, "secret") (i) Something unknown to the Jewish people and to the pagans but now revealed in the *Church.* The central mystery of the Christian faith is the mystery of *Easter* – the death and resurrection of Jesus Christ; (ii) often used to mean something beyond the power of human reason to work out, hence needing to be revealed by God; (iii) an aspect of the life of Christ chosen as a subject for *meditation*, especially in the *Rosary*.

Mystical Body of Christ Most commonly used to mean the *Church*, considered as being formed by the *Eucharist*, and forming the Eucharist. In the most ancient usage, the Mystical Body of Christ was the Eucharist; but in later times, it has often been used to refer to the Church.

N

Neocatechumenal Way (also called the **Neocatechumenate**) A way of formation in faith for small communities of baptized Christians or *catechumens*, on the model of the *catechumenate* of the early *Church*.

Neophyte (Greek *NEOPHUTOS*, "newly planted") A newly baptized Christian.

New Movements Various realities in the *Church* (*Neocatechumenate*, *Focolare* and others) that began during the late twentieth century and have flourished since the Second Vatican Council. *Opus Dei* is often referred to as a new movement although strictly speaking it is a Personal Prelature.

New Testament The *Gospels* and those other early Christian writings the *Church* has discerned to be part of the *Canon of Scripture*.

Nihil Obstat (Latin, "nothing hinders") Official statement by a qualified theologian (usually known as the Diocesan Censor) that a book or similar document contains nothing contrary to the teaching of the *Church*, preliminary to its being given an *Imprimatur*.

None (Latin *NONUS*, "ninth") The sixth hour of the older *Divine Office*, for the ninth hour after daybreak. See *Midday prayer*.

Norbertines See *Premonstratensians*.

Nôtre Dame French for *Our Lady*.

Novena (medieval Latin "ninth" from *NOVEM*, "nine") A prayer or devotion carried on for nine successive days, or weeks, or months. The prototype is the nine days between *Ascension* Thursday and *Pentecost* Sunday.

Novice A person received into a religious community but not yet formally or permanently vowed to the life. See *Postulant*.

Novitiate (i) The state of, or time spent, being a *novice*; (ii) a particular part of a religious house set aside for novices.

Nova Vulgata See *Vulgate*.

Novus Ordo Tendentious and often pejorative term for the reformed *Mass* of the Roman Rite; see *Mass of Paul VI*, *Ordinary Form*.

Nullity A declaration that what was supposed to be a valid marriage was not so. See *annulment*.

Nun (late Latin *NONNA*, "granny") A woman who lives a life of prayer, equivalent to a *monk*.

Nunc Dimittis (Latin, "now thou dost dismiss") The *Canticle* of Simeon (*Lk* 2:29-35), used at *Compline*.

Nuncio (Italianized form of Latin *NUNTIUS*, "messenger") A more formally established *Apostolic Delegate*.

Nunnery Older English usage for a convent of *nuns*.

Nuptial Mass (Latin *NUPTIALIS*, "of or concerning a wedding") *Mass* within which a couple celebrate the *Sacrament* of *Matrimony*; sometimes called a Wedding Mass.

O

Obedience As a religious virtue or *vow*, the commitment to follow the instructions of the superior of a *monastery* or other religious institution.

Oblate (Latin *OBLATUS* "something or someone offered") (i) In older monastic tradition, a boy entrusted by his parents to a *monastery* to be educated and eventually to become a *monk*; (ii) more recently, a *layperson* who has a formal affiliation with a particular *monastery*; (iii) a member of one of several *orders* of *clerks regular* (e.g. the Oblates of St Charles).

Octave (Latin *OCTAVUS*, "eighth") The custom of extending a major liturgical feast throughout the succeeding eight days, formerly kept for all *Solemnities*, now only *Christmas* and *Easter*.

Offertory (i) The action of presenting the bread and wine to be *consecrated* at *Mass*, hence the **Offertory Prayers** that go with this, and the **Offertory verse** sung to accompany it; (ii) the collection of money usually taken during the Offertory at Mass.

Office Familiar term for the *Divine Office*.

Office of Readings An alternative name for *Matins*.

Old Testament Traditional term for the Jewish *Scriptures*, first written in Hebrew or Greek, which form the bulk of the Bible.

Ombrellino (Italian, "small umbrella') A fabric umbrella carried over the *Blessed Sacrament* during indoor *processions*, e.g. on *Corpus Christi*.

Opening Prayer A term for the *Collect*.

Opus Dei (Latin "the work of God") (i) Traditional term for the *Divine Office*, especially as sung in *Benedictine monasteries*; (ii) an organization of *lay people* dedicated to growth in holiness, served by priests of the Society of the Holy Cross, and founded by St Josemaría Escrivá.

Oratory (i) A place of prayer which does not contain an *altar*; sometimes used for any *chapel*; (ii) a spiritual exercise of prayers, readings, preaching and music founded by St Philip Neri to help the *laity* to pray. The **Congregation of the Oratory** was instituted to conduct these exercises.

Order, Holy The various grades of service to God and the *Church*, originally consisting of seven orders; now confined to three, *Deacon*, *Priest* and *Bishop*, conferred by the *sacrament of ordination*.

Order, Religious A national or international organization of *monks*, *nuns*, *friars* etc dedicated to *prayer* or *mission*. Every order has its own distinctive *charism*.

Order of Mass The *Ordinary of the Mass*.

Ordination The *sacrament* of conferral of *Holy Order*. See *Order, Holy*.

Ordinary Form of the Roman Rite: the *Mass of Paul VI*, reformed after the Second Vatican Council. See also *Extraordinary Form*.

Ordinary of the Mass Those elements of the *Mass* that do not change whatever the liturgical season; sometimes called the *Order of Mass*. See *Proper*.

Ordinary Time "Ordinary" here means "numbered, ordered", from the Latin *ORDINARIUS*. It refers to those weeks of the liturgical year which do not fall within the seasons of *Advent*, *Christmas*, *Lent*, or *Easter*, and include a period of around 34 numbered weeks. Sometimes known as "Time through the Year".

Ordination Conferring the status of *deacon*, *priest* or *bishop* by prayer and the laying on of hands, to *consecrate* them for sacred duties; performed only by a bishop.

Original Sin The *dogma* that all human beings, apart from the *Virgin Mary*, are marked by a collective and inherited predisposition to sin as a result of the disobedience of our remote ancestors. See *Immaculate Conception*.

Orphrey (falsely inferred singular form of Middle English *ORPHREIS*, Old French *ORFREIS* from medieval Latin *AURIFRISIUM*, var of classical *AURIPHRYGIUM* "Phrygian gold, goldsmith's work") A strip of decorated fabric, used to adorn *vestments* such as the *chasuble* and *dalmatic*, and the *altar-frontal*.

Orthodoxy (Greek *ORTHODOXIA* "right belief" from *ORTHOS* "straight, right, correct" and *DOKEIN* "to believe") (i) The state of holding correct beliefs in matters of Christian *doctrine*; adj., **orthodox**; (ii) the *Orthodox Church*.

Orthodox Church Generic term for the various apostolic *churches* of the East, not in communion with the *Holy See* but preserving the *apostolic succession* and the *sacraments*. See *Filioque*.

Ostiarius (Latin "doorkeeper, ostiary" from *OSTIUM* "door"; forms with an initial *H-* are sometimes found, but are not standard). See *Porter*.

Our Father The prayer that Jesus taught to his *disciples* (*Mt* 6:9-13) See also *Pater noster*, *Lord's Prayer*.

Our Lady Common Catholic way of referring to the *Virgin Mary*.

Our Lord Common Catholic way of referring to Jesus Christ.

P

Pall (i) A small square of stiffened fabric, used to cover the *chalice* to keep dust and flies out of it; (ii) a large fabric cover to drape over a coffin, traditionally black. Hence **pall-bearers** who walk beside the coffin.

Palm A branch of palm or other greenery (traditionally the pussy-willow, but now usually a real palm frond). Palms, as an evergreen, are an ancient Christian symbol of the resurrection to eternal life.

Palm Sunday The Sunday beginning *Holy Week*, also known as *Passion Sunday* because on that day a *Gospel* account of Christ's Passion is read. Called Palm Sunday because traditionally on that day *palm* fronds are carried in *procession* to commemorate Jesus's triumphal entry into Jerusalem (*Mk* 11:1-10).

Paraclete (Greek *PARAKLETOS* "advocate") A title of the *Holy Spirit* (see *Jn* 16:5-11).

Paralipomena (Greek, *PARALEIPOMENA*, "those things that were omitted") The name in the *Septuagint* and *Vulgate* Bibles for the Books of Chronicles.

Parish (Middle English *PAROCHE*, *PARISSHE* from Latin *PAROCHIA*, *PAROECIA*, from Greek *PAROIKIA*, originally "sojourning" (from *PAROIKOS*, "stranger, sojourner", the condition of the Christian in this life), hence the Christian community primarily seen as a people in exile. Later it takes on a geographical sense, in a development that may also have yielded the form *PARK*, "enclosed land") The smallest unit of territory in the *Church*, centred on a single church and served by a *priest* as **Parish Priest** (in America, **Pastor**), often with one or more assistants or *curates*, living in a *presbytery*.

Parousia (Greek, "advent, arrival") Technical term for the *Second Coming*.

Pasch (Hebrew *PESACH*, "Passover") *Easter*; hence **Paschaltide**, the *Easter Season*, and **Paschal Candle**, a great candle blessed at the *Easter Vigil* and kept on the *sanctuary*, traditionally until the *Ascension*, now at least until *Pentecost* if not all year round.

Paschal Praeconium See *Exsultet*.

Passion The narrative of the suffering and death of Jesus, read solemnly on *Palm Sunday* and *Good Friday*.

Passion Sunday Formerly, the Sunday two weeks before *Easter*; now used as a synonym for *Palm Sunday*.

Passover The great Jewish festival, recalling the liberation from the bondage of Egypt by the mighty acts of God, when the Jewish people marked their doorposts with the blood of lambs. Understood by the *Church* as a type of our being set free from sin through the blood of Christ, the true Lamb of God. See *Easter*.

Pastoral letter A letter from a *bishop* to Christians in his *diocese*, usually read aloud at each *Mass* celebrated in that diocese on a given Sunday.

Pastoral staff See *crosier*.

Paten (Latin *PATINA*, Greek *PATANE* "shallow dish, plate") A plate of gold or gilt silver, used for the bread which is to be *consecrated* at *Mass*.

Pater noster (Latin "Our Father") Latin form of the *Lord's Prayer*.

Patristics Study of the *Church Fathers* (see *Fathers of the Church*).

Patron Saint A *saint* who is particularly honoured in a specific nation, city or parish, or by a particular group of people; e.g. Ss Cosmas and Damian for doctors, St George for England.

Peace, Sign of An action during *Mass* to symbolize, and effect, the unity and peace amongst the Christian community. Traditionally expressed by a "kiss" cheek to cheek; in England, a handshake is often substituted.

Pectoral Cross (Latin *PECTORALIS*, "of the chest" from *PECTUS* "chest, heart") A large *cross* worn displayed on the chest by a *bishop* or *abbot*.

Penance (Latin *PAENITENTIA*, "turning back") (i) The acceptance that we have failed by sin, and the firm resolve to make a fresh start, best expressed in the Sacrament of Penance or *Reconciliation*, usually called *confession*; (ii) a prayer recited, an action undertaken, or a suffering willingly accepted, to demonstrate the sincerity of sorrow for sin, and a wish to share in the saving work of Christ. Traditionally penance consists of *prayer*, *fasting* and *almsgiving*.

Penitential Liturgy A separate service, often during *Lent* or *Advent*, calling the Christian community to repentance and offering the chance for sacramental *confession*.

Penitential Rite A preliminary part of the *Mass* including an admission of guilt and confident prayer for forgiveness.

Penitential Psalms Seven *psalms* (6, 32, 38, 51, 102, 130, 143) expressing sorrow and repentance, frequently found in the context of *penitential liturgies*.

Pentecost (Greek *PENTEKOSTÉ*, "fiftieth") Sunday fifty days after Easter Sunday concluding the season of *Easter*. It commemorates the descent of the *Holy Spirit* on the *Apostles* and the *Virgin Mary* (*Ac* 2:1-13), which took place on the Jewish feast of Pentecost. This feast, fifty days after the first day of *Passover*, is also called the Feast of Weeks; as well as being a harvest festival, in Jewish tradition it also commemorates the revelation of the Torah (the Law) to Moses on Mount Sinai. The Holy Spirit's descent in the form of tongues of fire reminds us of God's descent in fire and smoke on Sinai (*Ex* 19:18).

Pericope (Greek *PERIKOPE*, "section, portion") Term used by Biblical scholars for a short passage of *Scripture*, especially from the *Gospels*.

Perpetual Succour, Our Lady of An image of the *Virgin Mary* and child Jesus that is the object of a particular devotion.

Peter's Pence Traditional English term for monetary offerings for the support of the *Holy See*.

Pontiff (Latin *PONTIFEX*, "bridge-builder" a title of some pagan priests in ancient Rome) A title of the *Pope* (Pontifex Maximus, the **Supreme Pontiff**), but also extended as an adjective, **pontifical**, to all *bishops*.

Pontifical The book containing the special ceremonies for which a *bishop* is responsible; see also *Ceremonial of Bishops*.

Poor Clares An *order* of *nuns* living in poverty, inspired by St Clare, the friend of St Francis.

Pope (Latin *PAPA*, "Pope, bishop" from Greek *PAPAS*, a formal variant of *PAPPAS* "daddy") The Bishop of Rome, successor of St Peter, chosen by the *Cardinals* to act as focus of unity and guarantee of truth for the entire *Church*.

Porter (late Latin *PORTARIUS*, from *PORTA* "door") Originally the fourth grade of *Holy Orders*, now suspended in the Latin Church. The responsibility was to guard the church door. The official name is *Ostiarius*.

Post-Communion Traditional term for the *Prayer after Communion* at *Mass*.

Postulation (i) the formal collection and presentation of evidence for a person's sanctity, collected preparatory to *beatification* or *canonization*; superintended by a **Postulator**; (ii) a period spent living in a vowed religious community (of *monks*, *nuns* or *friars*) whilst discerning whether to proceed to the *novitiate*. A person undertaking this exercise is known as a **postulant**.

Poverty Voluntary poverty understood as a religious virtue or vow; among *monks*, the commitment not to claim ownership of anything personally.

Praeconium, Paschal See *Exsultet*.

Prague, Infant of See *Infant of Prague*.

Prayer "Lifting up of heart and soul to God": both public, in the *Mass* and other ceremonies, and private. Private prayer may be vocal (using words) or mental; the latter either *meditative* or *contemplative*.

Prayer after Communion The prayer recited by the priest after *Communion* at *Mass*, formerly called the *Post-communion*.

Prayer of the Faithful The intercessions made at *Mass* after the *sermon*, often called *Bidding Prayers*.

Prayer over the Gifts The prayer recited by the *priest* after the *Offertory* at *Mass*, formerly called the *Secret*.

Preach (Latin *PRAEDICARE*, "proclaim") To deliver an authoritative address instructing the faithful, usually at *Mass* (see *sermon*, *homily*) The preserve of *priests* and *deacons*, most of whose long training is preparation for preaching.

Preface (Latin *PRAEFATIO*, "something spoken before") A thanksgiving prayer introducing the *Eucharistic Prayer* at *Mass*.

Prelate (Latin *PRAELATUS*, "someone put forward") A senior member of the *clergy*; some are nominally members of the Papal household (Prelates of Honour, Domestic Prelates, or *Protonotaries Apostolic*), usually known in England as *Monsignori*; *bishops* and *abbots* are also prelates.

Premonstratensians (Latin *PREMONSTRATENSIENSIS*, "from Prémontré [in France]") An order of *canons regular* founded by St Norbert, who wear white *habits*. Also called *Norbertines*.

Presbyter (Greek *PRESBUTEROS* "elder") Another term for a *priest*.

Presbytery (Greek *PRESBUTERION*, "presbyter's house") The house where the *parish priest* and *curates* live, adjacent to the parish church. In America known as a *rectory*.

Presentation of the Lord A *feast* on 2nd February (formerly called the *Purification*, or *Candlemas*), commemorating the Presentation of the child Jesus by his parents in the Temple (*Lk* 2:22-38).

Priest (Old English *PREOST*, from popular Latin **PRESTER*, var of *PRESBYTER*, from Greek *PRESBUTEROS*, "elder") A man set aside through *ordination* to serve God and the *Church*, with the particular power of hearing *confessions*, anointing the sick, and celebrating *Mass*. In the Western Church expected to be unmarried and to live in *celibacy*.

Prime (Latin *PRIMA* [*HORA*], "first hour") The third hour of the *Divine Office*, at the first hour of daylight, now generally omitted. See *Divine Office*; *Midday Prayer*.

Prior, Prioress The one in charge of a small *monastery* or **Priory**; also the second-in-command of a large *monastery* or *Abbey*.

Procession A devotional exercise consisting in people walking solemnly in line (processing), either around a *church* or from one church to another, sometimes carrying the *Blessed Sacrament*, or a statue or banners. Often a feature of the solemnity of *Corpus Christi*, certain Marian devotions, and *Good Friday*.

Promoter of the Faith An official of the *Curia* charged with presenting objections to a cause for *canonization* or *beatification*, or resolving controversies connected with it; sometimes known informally as the *Devil's Advocate*.

Proper Those elements of the *Mass* (prayers, *prefaces* &c) that vary according to the liturgical season. See *Ordinary of the Mass*.

Protonotary Apostolic (Medieval Latin *PROTONOTARIUS* "chief clerk", from Greek *PROTOS* "first" and Latin *NOTARIUS* "secretary") Originally a senior secretary to the *Pope*, now the highest grade of honorary *prelate* or *monsignor* below a *bishop*.

Province An area of territory consisting of several *dioceses*, headed by an *Archbishop*.

Provost (Old English *PROFOST*, Medieval Latin *PROPOSITUS*, Latin *PRAEPOSITUS*, "set in charge") The superior of a community of *canons*, or a Congregation of the *Oratory*.

Psalm (Greek *PSALMOS* "song accompanied by the harp" from *PSALLEIN* "to pluck, to sing with harp accompanying") One of the one hundred and fifty Hebrew prayer-poems forming the Scriptural Book of Psalms. They remain a central part of Christian worship, especially in the *Divine Office*.

Pulpit (Latin *PULPITUM* "platform") A high raised platform, with enclosing rail, for preaching, situated so that the preacher is easily visible from all parts of the church.

Purgatory (Medieval Latin *PURGATORIUM* "place of cleansing") The state of souls after death who still need to be cleansed from disordered attachments and to expiate the punishment owing for sin, before coming to the sight of God face to face that is the fullness of joy in heaven; prayer for the souls in Purgatory (the *Holy Souls*), which aids them in this, is a duty of the Christian and one of the *Spiritual Works of Mercy*. See *indulgence*.

Purification (i) The process of cleaning the *paten* and *chalice* after *Mass*, to ensure that no crumbs or drops of the *Eucharist* remain. The chalice is wiped and dried with a **Purificator**, a white folded rectangle of linen; (ii) the traditional name for the feast on 2nd February, commemorating the ceremony when Mary came to give thanks for her childbirth, and the infant Jesus was presented in the Temple; otherwise called *Candlemas*.

Pyx (Latin *PYXIS*, Greek *PUXIS* "box") A small round airtight container, often made of precious metal, for carrying a consecrated *Host* to give *Communion* to the sick.

Q

Quadragesima (Latin "fortieth") The season of *Lent*, comprising forty days until *Easter*.

Quarant'ore Italian for *Forty Hours* devotion.

Quasimodo Sunday (Latin, "in the manner of") The Sunday after *Easter Sunday* when the *introit* begins "in the manner of new born infants" and thus named. In England called *Low Sunday*.

Quinquagesima (Latin "fiftieth") In the older liturgical calendar, the last Sunday before *Lent*, fifty days before *Holy Saturday*.

R

RCIA Abbreviation of *Rite of Christian Initiation of Adults*, properly the title of a book of ceremonies for receiving adult converts; commonly used to mean the *catechumenate*.

Reconciliation The process of making up differences, forgiving and being forgiven. Refers also to the **Sacrament of Reconciliation**, or of *Penance*, also known as *confession*.

Rector (Latin "ruler") A little-used word for a *priest* with responsibility for a church; in America **rectory** is commonly used for a *presbytery*. The head of a *seminary* is usually called a rector.

Regulars (Latin *REGULARIS*, "concerning a Rule") A name for those *clergy* who belong to religious *orders*; see *Seculars*.

Relic Material remains of a *saint* or *beatified* person, used as a *sacramental*. There are three classes of relics: a first-class relic is a part of the body of the saint or *blessed*; a second-class relic, something (such as a garment) used by them during their lifetime; a third-class relic something that has been touched to their remains after their death.

Religious (Latin *RELIGIOSUS* from *RELIGIO*, "binding together") Members of an order of *monks*, *nuns*, *friars* etc, as distinguished from *secular clergy*. See *order*, *religious*.

Reliquary A container used to house and often to display a *relic* of a *saint*.

Remembrance Sunday In England and Wales, the Sunday closest to November 11th, where particular remembrance is made of those who have died in war, especially the two World Wars of the twentieth century.

Requiem (Latin, "rest") A *Mass* for the Dead, named after the first word in the *introit*.

Reservation of the Blessed Sacrament Keeping some of the consecrated *Eucharist* in the form of bread in a *Tabernacle*, so that it is available for *Communion* of the sick, and for *adoration*.

Responsorial Psalm A *psalm* sung or recited antiphonally after the first reading at *Mass*.

Retreat Time, often of several days' duration, devoted to *prayer* and reflection, often spent at a *monastery* or similar location.

RIP Abbreviation of the Latin Requiescat in pace, "may he [or she] rest in peace" – a brief prayer for the dead.

Rite of Christian Initiation of Adults See *RCIA*.

Rochet (Old French, "small coat") A garment similar to a *surplice* but with narrow *sleeves*; worn by *canons* and *prelates*.

Rogation Days (Latin *ROGATIO* "a request" from *ROGARE* "to ask") In the old liturgical calendar, special days of penitential prayer marked with outdoor processions, originally to ask for a successful harvest. Four were celebrated: St Mark's Day (April 25th) and the three days before *Ascension*. Now replaced by days of prayer for particular needs determined by local *bishops*.

Roman Catholic Since the seventeenth century, the formal legal description of Catholics under English Law; in itself it is a tautology, and should not be used by Catholics to describe themselves.

Rosary (Latin *ROSARIUM* "rose garden") A traditional form of prayer to the *Virgin Mary*. It is usually recited on a *chaplet* of beads (called **rosary beads**, or often just a rosary). Its basic pattern is called a decade (each one *Our Father*, ten *Hail Marys*, and one *Glory Be*). Each decade is assigned to a particular episode (called a *mystery*) from the *New Testament*, dealing with the life of Christ and the *Virgin Mary*, which is meditated on whilst the prayers are said. There are twenty mysteries in all, arranged in four groups of five (Joyful, Luminous, Sorrowful, and Glorious).

Rubric (Latin, *RUBRICUS*, from *RUBER* "red") Instructions, traditionally printed in red letters, in liturgical books giving instructions about what the *priest* and ministers should *do*; whilst what they should *say* is printed in black.

S

Sabaoth A Hebrew title given to God, of uncertain meaning; sometimes rendered "[Lord God] of Hosts", but often left untranslated.

Sabbath Originally the seventh day of the Jewish week (Saturday) marked by refraining from work, by festive meals, and by meditation on *Scripture*, to commemorate God's rest after the six days of creation. Christians celebrate the Sabbath on Sunday, the first day of the week, the day of Christ's resurrection, above all with the *Eucharist*.

Sacrament (Latin *SACRAMENTUM*, originally "solemn engagement, military oath" from *SACRARE*, "consecrate"; subsequently used to translate Greek *MUSTERION* "secret thing, ceremony") One of seven ceremonies (efficacious signs) instituted by Christ and used in the *Church* to bring people into contact with God in different ways: *Baptism* and *Confirmation* as initiation, *Eucharist* for incorporation into the Body of Christ, and for regular nourishment; *Ordination* or *Matrimony* for Christian mission, *Penance* and *Anointing of the Sick* for when things go wrong.

Sacrament of the Sick See *anointing of the sick*.

Sacramental A sacred sign analogous to the *sacraments* by which spiritual benefits are obtained through the prayers of the *Church*. They include gestures (blessings, kneeling, the *Sign of the Cross*) and blessed objects (*vestments*, *chaplets*, medals, *scapulars*, *crucifixes*, *holy water*, blessed oils and others).

Sacramentary A book containing the various prayers for *Mass* without the Bible readings (see *Lectionary*); also called an *Altar Missal*. See also *Missal*.

Sacred Heart of Jesus A devotion celebrating the human love of God for us, expressed in the heart of Jesus. Commemorated with a *Solemnity* on Friday after the second Sunday after *Pentecost*.

Saint (Old French *SEINT*, *SAINT* from Latin *SANCTUS* "holy")
A particular Christian who has lived a life of heroic virtue and
to whose posthumous intercession miracles are attributed, who
has been officially declared worthy of veneration by the
universal *Church* as an intercessor and an example of holiness.
See *canonization*.

Saint Joseph Spouse of the *Virgin Mary*, and *patron* of the
universal Church and of Christian fatherhood; *Solemnity* on
19th March.

Saint Peter and Saint Paul St Peter, *Apostle* and first *Pope*; St
Paul, great evangelizer ("Apostle to the Gentiles") and author of
many of the *New Testament* letters; traditionally considered as
founders of the *church* in Rome. Commemorated by a *Solemnity*
on 29th June; a *Holy Day of Obligation*.

Saints' days Days commemorating particular saints, usually the
anniversary of the day they died; major ones are commemorated
world-wide, as *Solemnities*, *Feasts* or *Memorials*; others have
only local commemorations. On every day of the year there are
many saints to commemorate, so not all can be kept anywhere.
See *Martyrology*, *feast-day*.

Salve Regina (Latin, "Hail [Holy] Queen") The Latin version
of the *Hail Holy Queen*, often sung.

Sanctuary The area of a *church* around the *altar*, set aside for
ceremonial worship; traditionally demarcated by steps and
altar-rails.

Sanctuary lamp A white or red lamp kept burning near the *tabernacle* to indicate that the *Blessed Sacrament* is reserved there.

Sanctus (Latin, "holy") Hymn-like text, beginning with "sanctus" (or "holy") sung or said thrice, between the *Preface* and the *Eucharistic Prayer* at *Mass*; often set to music.

Scapular (Latin *SCAPULARE*, "a shoulder covering" from *SCAPULA* "shoulder") Originally a piece of cloth worn over the shoulders as part of a religious *habit*, a scapular now generally refers to two small pieces of cloth, inscribed with various markings, worn on a cord around the neck as a *sacramental*. There are various different types of scapular; the best known is the **brown scapular** of the *Carmelites*.

Schism (Greek *SCHISMA*, "a rent, tear" from *SCHIZO* "to split, part") The formal and deliberate separation of a group of Christians from the unity of the *Church*; the initial reason for the split is usually disciplinary rather than *doctrinal*. See *heresy*.

Scripture Usual Catholic term for the Holy Bible.

Scrutiny The ceremonial examination of *catechumens* before *Baptism*, sometimes conducted publicly on Sundays in *Lent*.

Seasons, liturgical Times during the *Church's* year when Christians particularly meditate on certain aspects of salvation: these are now *Advent*, the season of *Christmas*, *Lent*, and *Eastertide*; plus *Ordinary Time*.

Second Coming The *Church's* belief that Jesus Christ will come again at the end of time (the *Parousia*).

Secret Old name for the *Prayer over the Gifts*; in the *Extraordinary Form* of *Mass* always said silently.

Seculars (Latin *SAECULARIS* from *SAECULUM*, "world") Generally, those in the world; in particular *priests* who have a mission to the world, who do not belong to a religious *order*.

Sede Vacante (Latin, "the see being vacant") used of a particular *diocese*, or the Papacy, to describe a period of hiatus in the tenure of the office between the death or resignation of one *bishop* and the appointment of another.

See (Latin *SEDES*, "seat") The seat of a *bishop*, hence his *diocese*. The *Holy See* is the Diocese of Rome.

Seminary (Latin *SEMINARIUM*, "seed bed", from *SEMINARE*, "to sow seed") A training college for *priests*, ideally situated adjacent to the *cathedral* and the *bishop's* residence. A **Junior Seminary** (in America, **Minor Seminary**) is for boys who would otherwise be unable to receive adequate education in adolescence; a **Major Seminary** for those over 18.

Septuagesima (Latin "seventieth") In the older liturgical calendar, the Sunday three weeks before *Lent*, seventy days before *Low Sunday*.

Septuagint (Latin, *SEPTUAGINTA* "seventy") The Greek translation of the *Old Testament*, traditionally the work of seventy scholars. Often abbreviated LXX.

Sequence (Latin *SEQUENTIA* "something following after [the Epistle]") A long hymn in accentual verse or rhythmic prose sung before the *Gospel* at *Mass* on certain special days.

Seraph, pl **Seraphim** (Hebrew *SARAPH*, pl *SERAPHIM*) One of the orders of *angels* recognized by tradition, usually represented as six-winged. See *cherub*, *angel*.

Sermon (Latin *SERMO*, "speech") A discourse in which the *priest* explains the readings at *Mass*; often called a *homily*.

Seven Sorrows of Mary Seven sorrowful events in the life of the *Virgin Mary* (the prophecy of Simeon (*Lk* 2:35), the flight into Egypt (*Mt* 2:13), the loss of the child Jesus in the Temple (*Lk* 2:46), the *Way of the Cross*, the Crucifixion, the descent from the Cross, and the entombment of Jesus); often the subject of *meditation*. See *Dolour Rosary*.

Sexagesima (Latin "sixtieth") In the older liturgical calendar, the Sunday two weeks before *Lent*, sixty days before Easter Wednesday.

Sext (Latin *SEXTUS*, "sixth") The fifth hour of the older *Divine Office*, for the sixth hour after daybreak, or midday. See *Midday prayer*.

Shrove Tuesday (Middle English *SCHRIFAN*, "make confession", Old English *SCRIFAN*, "impose a penance" from Latin *SCRIBERE* "to write", since penances were once given formally in writing) The day before *Ash Wednesday*, when Catholics traditionally receive the *Sacrament of Penance* as a preparation for *Lent*. Historically marked by using up the meat and dairy products from which people fasted, and therefore called "fat Tuesday" (Mardi gras), or "goodbye meat"(carne vale, carnival).

Side Altar A subsidiary *altar* in a large *church*.

Side Chapel The area around a *side altar*.

Sign of the Cross The most common Christian *sacramental* gesture, in which one touches first the head then the torso then each of the shoulders, usually whilst reciting "In the name of the Father and the Son and the Holy Spirit".

Sisters of Bethlehem An order of *contemplative nuns*, broadly *Carthusian* in their *charism*; founded in 1950 and now spread worldwide. There is also an affiliated order of *monks*.

Society of Jesus (SJ) See *Jesuit*.

Society of St Vincent de Paul (SVP) An association of *lay people* devoted to practical works of charity.

Sodality (Latin *SODALITAS*, "companionship") An organisation promoting pious or charitable acts, such as prayer for *vocations*.

Solemnity The highest rank of special days, for really important *saints* (including the local *patron*), and events in the life of Jesus. See *feast-day*, *memorial*.

Soutane (French, from Italian *SOTTANA* "undergarment") See *cassock*.

Special Minister A widely used but incorrect term for an *Extraordinary Minister of Holy Communion*.

Sphragis (Greek, "seal") The *sign of the cross* made on the forehead, particularly of a *catechumen* as part of *baptism*, to claim the person for Christ (see *Rv* 7:2-3).

Spiritual Exercises A book of structured *meditations* written by St Ignatius Loyola (founder of the *Jesuit* order).

Spiritual Works of Mercy Seven types of action appropriate for the Christian: converting the sinner, instructing the ignorant, counselling the doubtful, comforting the sorrowful, bearing wrongs patiently, forgiving injustice, praying for the living and the dead. See also *Corporal Works of Mercy*.

Sponsor A mature Christian who presents a candidate for *Baptism* or *Confirmation* and undertakes responsibility for his or her growth in the Faith.

Stations of the Cross (Latin *STATIO*, "stopping place") A devotion following in imagination the walk of Jesus from the court of Pontius Pilate to the hill of Calvary, with fourteen "stations" based on sites in Jerusalem where certain events are believed to have occurred. Representations or symbols of the Stations are usually arranged around the walls of churches. See *Way of the Cross*.

Stigmata (Greek, "markings") The marks of one or more of the wounds of Christ appearing on the body of a devout person. Of themselves they are no indication of holiness, although several *saints* (most famously St Francis and Padre Pio) have exhibited them.

Stole (Latin *STOLA* from Greek *STOLÉ*, "garment") The fifth of the *vestments* for *Mass*, a band of fabric, usually fringed, and of a colour and design to match the *chasuble* (and *maniple*, if used), worn round the neck and hanging down in front. Traditionally it was crossed on the breast, except by *bishops*. It is worn over the left shoulder by *deacons*. Also used over a *surplice* when administering the sacraments of *Baptism*,

Penance and *Anointing*. A miniature stole is used for administering *Communion* and Anointing in homes or hospitals. Its origins are unclear but probably lie in the scarf of office worn by Roman Imperial officials.

Subdeacon A grade of *Holy Order* below *deacon*, at present suspended in the Western Church.

Succession, Apostolic See *Apostolic Succession*.

Surplice (Anglo-Norman *SURPLIS*, Old French *SOURPLIS* from medieval Latin *SUPERPELLICIUM* [sc *VESTIMENTUM*], "something worn over fur garments") A light garment of white fabric with wide sleeves, closed at the front, worn over the *cassock*.

SVP The *Society of St Vincent de Paul*.

Synod (Greek *SUNODOS*, "assembly, meeting") A meeting of *bishops*, usually for one nation or region (local Synod). The **Synod of Bishops** meets regularly in Rome as an advisory body to the *Pope*.

Synoptic Gospels (Greek *SUNOPTIKOS*, "seen all at once") The first three *Gospels*, Matthew Mark and Luke, share many passages in common. Various theories, none of them entirely satisfactory, have been proposed to explain this. These Gospels are nevertheless frequently known as "the Synoptics" in allusion to these parallel passages.

T

Tabernacle (Latin *TABERNACULUM*, "tent") A secure strong fixed container in a *church* or *chapel* for reserving the *Blessed*

Sacrament, indicated by a *sanctuary lamp* and covered with a **tabernacle veil** of the colour of the *season*.

Tantum Ergo (Latin "[Bowing before] so great [a sacrament], therefore") Opening words of a thirteenth century Latin hymn to the *Blessed Sacrament*, written by St Thomas Aquinas and typically sung at *Benediction*.

Te Deum (Latin, "[we praise] You, O God") Opening words of a fourth century hymn of praise, probably originally composed for the *Easter Vigil*. Sung at the end of the *Office of Readings* on Sundays and great *feast-days*, and also on occasions of particular thanksgiving.

Tenebrae (Latin, "darkness") Old name for *Matins* and *Lauds* of *Maundy Thursday*, *Good Friday* and *Holy Saturday*, formerly sung in darkness with dramatic effect.

Terce (Latin *TERTIUS*, "third") The fourth hour of the older *Divine Office*, for the third hour after daybreak. See *Midday prayer*.

Theological Virtues Faith, Hope, Love (see 1 *Co* 13:13).

Theotokos (Greek, "God-bearer") Title of the *Virgin Mary*, found as early as the third century AD, formally defined at the Council of Ephesus in 431; expresses the *dogma* that she gave birth to Jesus Christ, true God and true man, and can be venerated as Mother of God.

Thurible (Latin *T(H)URIBULUM*, from *THUS*, Greek *THYOS* "incense") A metal container suspended from chains, used for burning *incense*. See *censer*.

Thurifer (Latin, "incense bearer") An *acolyte* entrusted with the *thurible* at *Mass*.

Tonsure (Latin *TONSURA*, "shaving") Shaving part of the head, usually the crown; originally the distinguishing mark of all *clergy*, now used only among certain orders of *monks* and *friars*.

Tract (Latin *TRACTUS* "something extended") In the older (*Tridentine*) liturgy, a text from *Scripture* sung before the *Gospel* during *Lent*, in place of the *Alleluia*.

Tradition (Latin *TRADITIO*, from *TRADERE*, "pass on") The duty of faithfully passing on to the next generation what we have received from the past (*Ti* 1:9), hence the ever-developing body of Catholic teaching, or *deposit of faith*. See also *Apostolic Tradition*.

Transfiguration A feast kept on 6th August to celebrate the Transfiguration of Jesus (Mk 9:2-8).

Tridentine Rite (Latin, *TRIDENTINUS* "from Trent") Frequently found name for the older form of the *Mass* of the Roman Rite prior to the reforms after the Second Vatican Council. Also called the Old Rite, classical Rite, Traditional Latin Mass (TLM), *Extraordinary Form*, *Mass of John XXIII*.

Triduum (Latin "three days") Three days at the end of *Holy Week* during which the entire *Easter* mystery is celebrated in its fullness in an extended series of liturgies from *Maundy Thursday* to *Good Friday*, *Holy Saturday* and the *Easter Vigil*. The greatest feast in the Christian calendar.

Trinity, Holy The mystery of the Godhead, Three Persons in One Nature.

Trinity Sunday The first Sunday after *Pentecost*, a *Solemnity* to meditate on the nature of God, Three in One.

Trinity Term The summer term at older English academic institutions, so called because *Trinity Sunday* typically fell within it.

Tunicle (Latin *TUNICULA*, "little tunic") A garment almost identical to the *dalmatic*, worn by the *subdeacon* at *High Mass*.

U

Unction, Extreme Old name for the *Anointing of the Sick*; see *last sacraments*.

V

Vatican A hill near Rome, the usual residence of the *Pope*. Although wholly surrounded by the city of Rome proper, it is in fact a separate sovereign state, formally the Vatican City State, with its own laws, police force, armed forces, post office &c. Also used as shorthand or casually to refer to the *Papacy* or *Holy See*.

Veni Creator (Latin, "come, creator [Spirit]") Hymn to the *Holy Spirit* often sung at *confirmations* and *ordinations*, or at *Pentecost*.

Veni Sancte Spiritus (Latin, "come, Holy Spirit") A *sequence* addressed to the *Holy Spirit*, sung at *Pentecost*.

Venial Sin (Latin *VENIALIS* "forgiveable") Strictly, any sin that is not a *mortal sin*: a sin involving objectively less serious matter, or done without full knowledge of its gravity, or by one whose freedom of choice has been involuntarily impaired. See *mortal sin*.

Vespers (Latin *VESPERAE*, "evening") The seventh hour of the *Divine Office*, also known as *Evening Prayer*; contains *psalms*, *canticles* from the *New Testament*, and the *Magnificat* or Canticle of Mary.

Vessels, Sacred The *chalice* and *paten* used at *Mass*.

Vestments (Latin *VESTIMENTA* "garments") The garments worn by *clergy* and assistants for *Mass* and other ceremonies. A full set of vestments comprises the *chasuble*, *stole*, *maniple*, *burse*, *chalice veil*, *tabernacle veil*, *lectern fall* and *altar-frontal*, supplemented with *dalmatic*, *tunicle* and *humeral veil* to make a traditional "*High Mass* set".

Via dolorosa (Latin, "sorrowful way") The *Way of the Cross*.

Viaticum (Latin, "food for the journey") The *sacrament* of *Holy Communion* given to those about to die.

Vicar (Latin *VICARIUS*, "substitute, deputy") An official with delegated authority. A **Vicar Apostolic** is delegated by the *Pope* to serve an area which has not been structured as a *diocese*; a **Vicar General** is the *bishop's* deputy for all matters, a **Vicar Judicial** his deputy for legal matters, whilst a **Vicar Episcopal** may look after an area within a diocese.

Vicar Forane See *dean*.

Vigil, Vigils (Latin *VIGILIAE*, "keeping watch") Generally, a vigil is praying during the night. Vigils is a name for the hour of *Matins* (the *Office of Readings* from the *Divine Office*) used by some monastic orders (such as the *Carthusians*) who celebrate it during the night. See also *Easter Vigil*, *Vigil Mass*.

Vigil Mass *Mass* for a Sunday or *feast* day celebrated on the evening beforehand; this expresses the *Church's* understanding of time, drawn from the Jewish tradition, whereby a day runs from sunset to sunset (thus, Sunday begins liturgically on Saturday evening).

Virgin Birth The *dogma* that Mary conceived and gave birth to Jesus Christ whilst remaining a virgin.

Virgin Mary See *Our Lady*, *Theotokos*, *Blessed Virgin Mary*.

Visitation A *feast* kept on 31st May to commemorate the visit of the *Virgin Mary* to her cousin Elizabeth (*Lk* 1:39-56).

Vocation (Latin *VOCATIO* "calling") The specific state of life to which an individual Christian is called by God. Every Christian has a vocation. *Marriage* and the *celibate* life are vocations; often used more narrowly to refer to a call to the *priesthood* or *religious life*.

Vow A solemn promise made to God before witnesses.

Vulgate (Latin, *[BIBLIA] VULGATA*, "[Bible] in common use") Usual term for St Jerome's translation and revision of the Bible in Latin, completed in the fifth century. The official text of the Catholic Bible is still in Latin, but has recently been revised in light of contemporary scholarship. This text is called the New Vulgate (*Nova Vulgata*).

W

Way of the Cross The path taken by Jesus to Calvary; sometimes used to mean the *Stations of the Cross*.

Whitefriars Traditional English name for *Carmelite friars*.

Whitsun, Whitsunday Traditional English name for *Pentecost*; the season of Pentecost was **Whitsuntide**.

Z

Zucchetto (Italian *ZUCHETTA*, "small gourd, cap") A round skull cap, black for *priests*, purple for *prelates*, red for *cardinals* and white for the *Pope*.